Read! Write! Discuss! Learn!

A Workbook of Interactive Handouts to Support the College Literacy Course

Mary Ann Gray-Schlegel
and
Yvonne M. King

On the cover: Image of children © 2008 by MaszaS. Used under license from Shutterstock, Inc.; notebook image © JupiterImages Corporation.

Title page image © 2008 by Jamie Duplass. Used under license from Shutterstock, Inc.

Copyright © 2008 by Mary Ann Gray-Schlegel and Yvonne M. King

ISBN 978-0-7575-5634-0

Kendall/Hunt Publishing Company has the exclusive rights to reproduce this work, to prepare derivative works from this work, to publicly distribute this work, to publicly perform this work and to publicly display this work.

All rights reserved. No part of this publication may be reproduced, stored in a retrieval system, or transmitted, in any form or by any means, electronic, mechanical, photocopying, recording, or otherwise, without the prior written permission of the copyright owner.

Printed in the United States of America

10 9 8 7 6

Dedication

It is with deep gratitude that we dedicate this handbook to our graduate students, offered us much insight and many ideas over the years. Their enthusiasm and passi eracy education have been our inspiration.

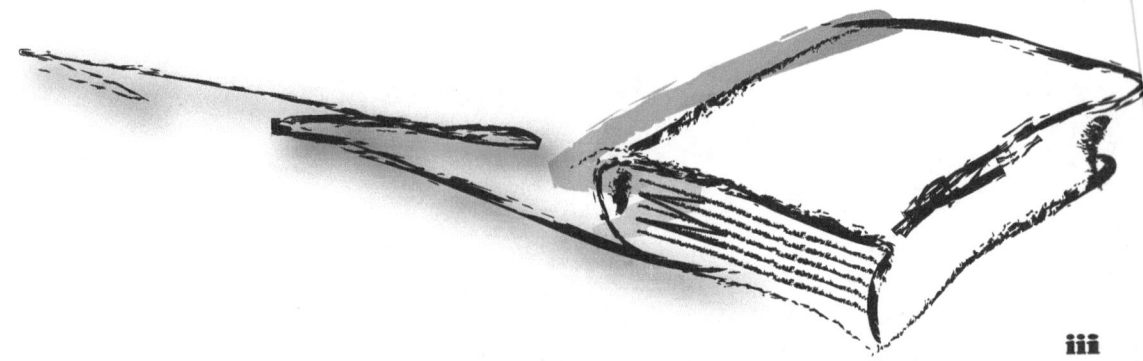

Contents

Introduction vii

Chapter 1   Balanced Literacy 1

Chapter 2   Approaches to Literacy Instruction 9

Chapter 3   Early Literacy 15

Chapter 4   Phonological Awareness 29

Chapter 5   Word Identification 35

Chapter 6   Fluency 47

Chapter 7   Vocabulary and Concept Development 55

Chapter 8   Comprehension 69

Chapter 9   Questioning 95

Chapter 10 Reading in the Content Areas 101

Chapter 11 The Reading-Writing Connection 109

Chapter 12 Literacy Assessment 121

Chapter 13 Diverse Learners 131

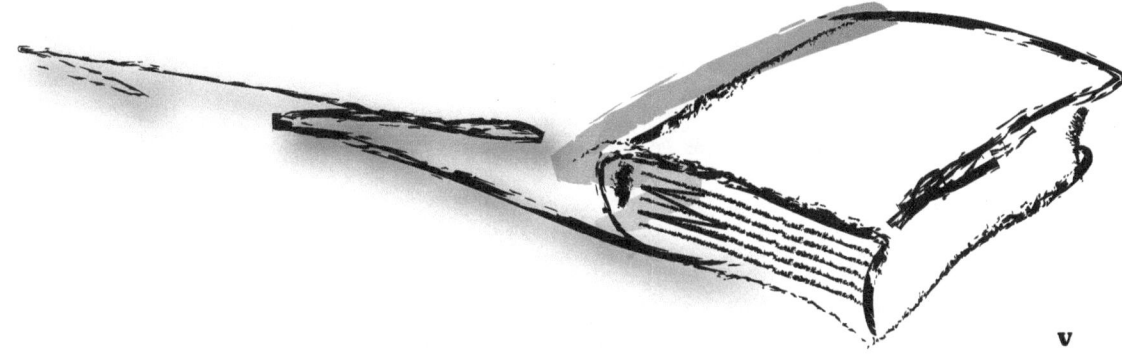

Contents

Introduction iv

Chapter 1   Balanced Literacy 1

Chapter 2   Approaches to Literacy Instruction 8

Chapter 3   Early Literacy 15

Chapter 4   Phonological Awareness 20

Chapter 5   Word Identification 26

Chapter 6   Fluency 47

Chapter 7   Vocabulary and Concept Development 55

Chapter 8   Comprehension 69

Chapter 9   Questioning 85

Chapter 10   Studying the Content Areas 107

Chapter 11   The Reading/Writing Connection 139

Chapter 12   Literary Elements 177

Chapter 13   Dictionaries 211

Introduction

Time does pass, but some things remain timeless. For more than 21 years, we have both taught an undergraduate foundations of reading course at the same university. Our students are majoring in early childhood education, upper elementary/middle level education, special education, or a combination. For most, our course is their first look at the discipline of reading education. Each semester, we watch as our students excitedly and yet with some trepidation approach the prospect of learning how to help their future students read and learn to read better. We observe them grappling with complex understandings of how literacy develops and what their role will be in that process. We also recognize that many times they become overwhelmed and sometimes frustrated by the sheer amount of new literacy concepts and vocabulary.

As university literacy instructors, we espouse a common philosophy about learning. Both of us firmly believe that learning is a social, constructive process. After all our years at this level, we have seen repeated evidence that our students understand better when we invite them to "mess around" with the material, to try out new ideas, discuss them with a peer, and process through writing or further discussion. We know that if we can activate any prior knowledge they might have on a topic and motivate them to use that background knowledge, their understandings will be richer, deeper, and more personally meaningful. It is not only through lecture and notetaking that education is shared, but through the hands-on activities and techniques that mentally engage their minds and their attitudes.

This handbook is a compilation of worksheets that we have gathered over the years to supplement a basic foundations of reading text. It is not an appendage to a specific course text; rather, it has been designed to supplement any chosen text due to its universal topics. Pages are perforated for ease in tearing some out and turning them in for quick accountability gauges. Graphic organizers are plentiful and diverse. Critical analysis of various topics is infused throughout. Select articles have been included from respected journals to broaden students' awareness of the literature. It is a consumable text—a working handbook—to guide students through the exciting and eye-opening journey into the world of literacy. Hop aboard!

Mary Ann Gray-Schlegel
Yvonne King
Summer, 2008

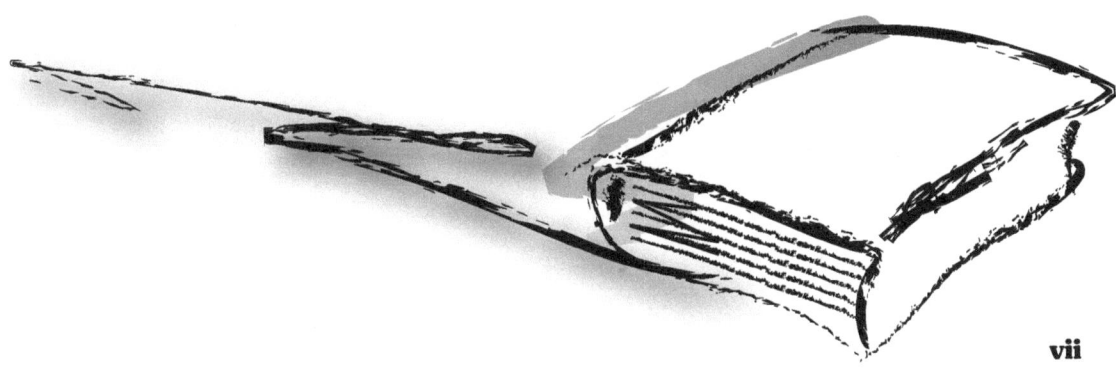

Chapter 1

Balanced Literacy

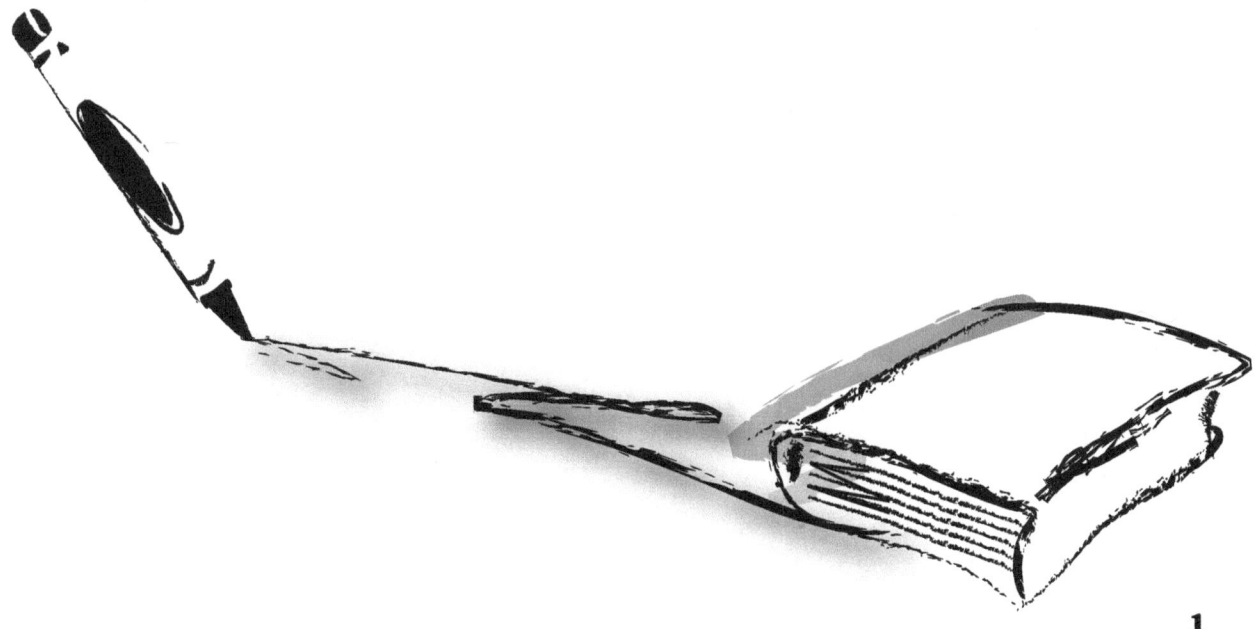

Balanced Literacy

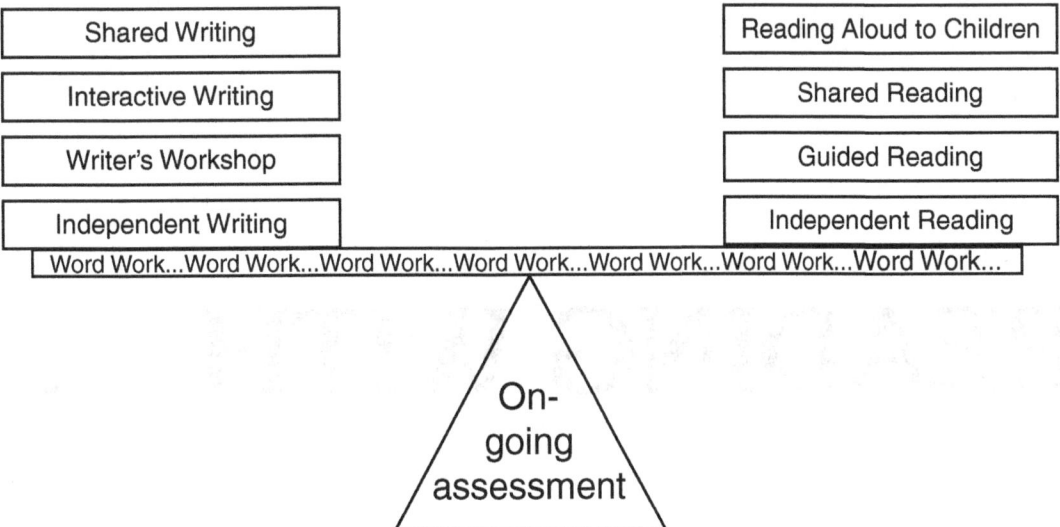

Every Day—Every Child!!

READING TO . . .

READING WITH . . .

READING BY . . .

EVERY DAY!!!

Major Elements of Balanced Reading Programs

Reading TO Children

- Teacher Reads Aloud
- Small-Group or One-to-One Reading

Reading WITH Children

- Shared Book Experience
- Shared Rhythm and Singing Experience
- Supported Reading (Choral, Echo, Shadow Reading)
- Language Experience
- Guided Reading

Reading BY Children

- Readers' Theater
- Sustained Silent Reading (SSR)/Independent Reading
- School and Class Libraries

Ray Reutzel and Robert Cooter (2008). *Teaching Children to Read: The Teacher Makes the Difference,* 5e. Upper Saddle River: Pearson/Merrill Prentice Hall, 2008.

How a Child Reads

Reader-Based Explanations ←——— Interactive Explanations ———→ Text-Based Explanations

Text: Throw it in the bushel

Child: Throw it in the basket

Teacher Response:

    Bottom-Up _____

    Interactive _____

    Top-Down _____

Shawn's footsteps slowed as he approached the open door. He double checked the number on the outside—104—and compared it to the paper he gripped in his hand. Excited children were pushing past him, yelling "Hello" and "Welcome back!" and "How was your summer?" to each other. A few glanced at him curiously but said nothing. Shawn pressed his notebooks to his chest, swallowed hard, and went in.

He chose an empty seat in the back of the room, near the wall maps and globe. Just then, a woman strode into the room. "Good morning, Ladies and Gentlemen" she announced briskly, "and welcome to second period. I'm sure we will have a productive year together!"

What is happening?

What were some "clues" that you used?

How does schema support comprehension?

Focused Literacy Conversation

- How did you learn to read?

- What home reading experiences do you remember?

- What did elementary teachers do that effectively helped you learn to read?

- What did teachers do that negatively affected your reading?

- Do you like to read? Why or why not?

Chapter 2

Approaches to Literacy Instruction

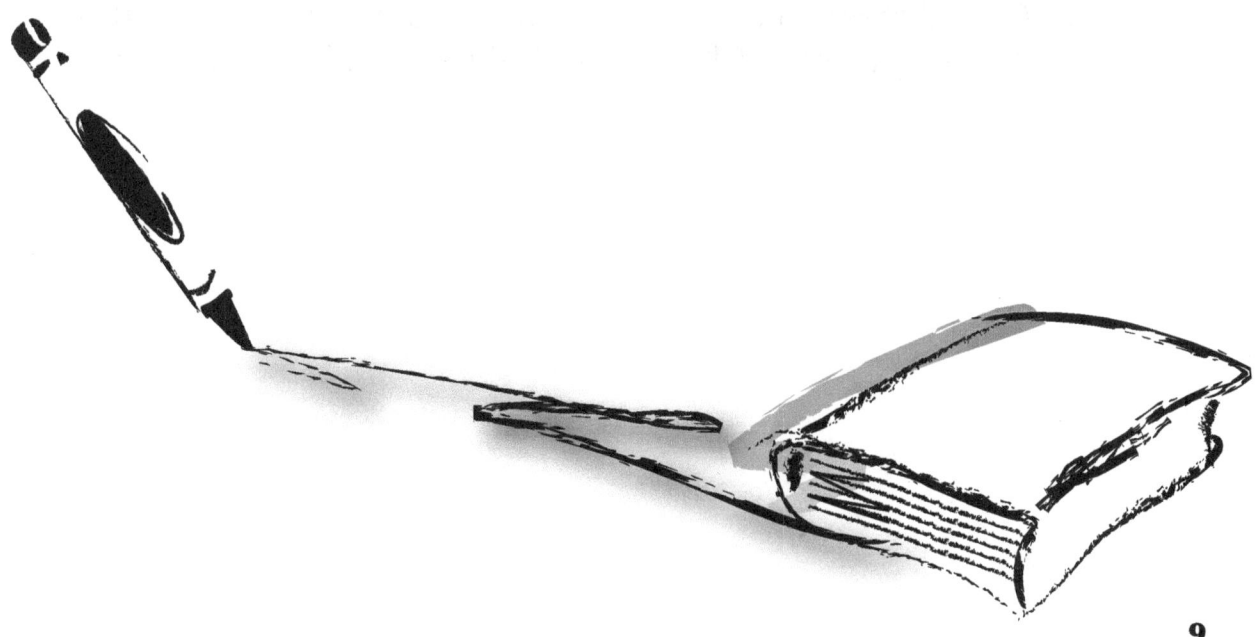

What Do You Remember?

Mark B-U to represent a Bottom-Up perspective of reading, T-D to signify a Top-Down perspective, and I if it is Interactive.

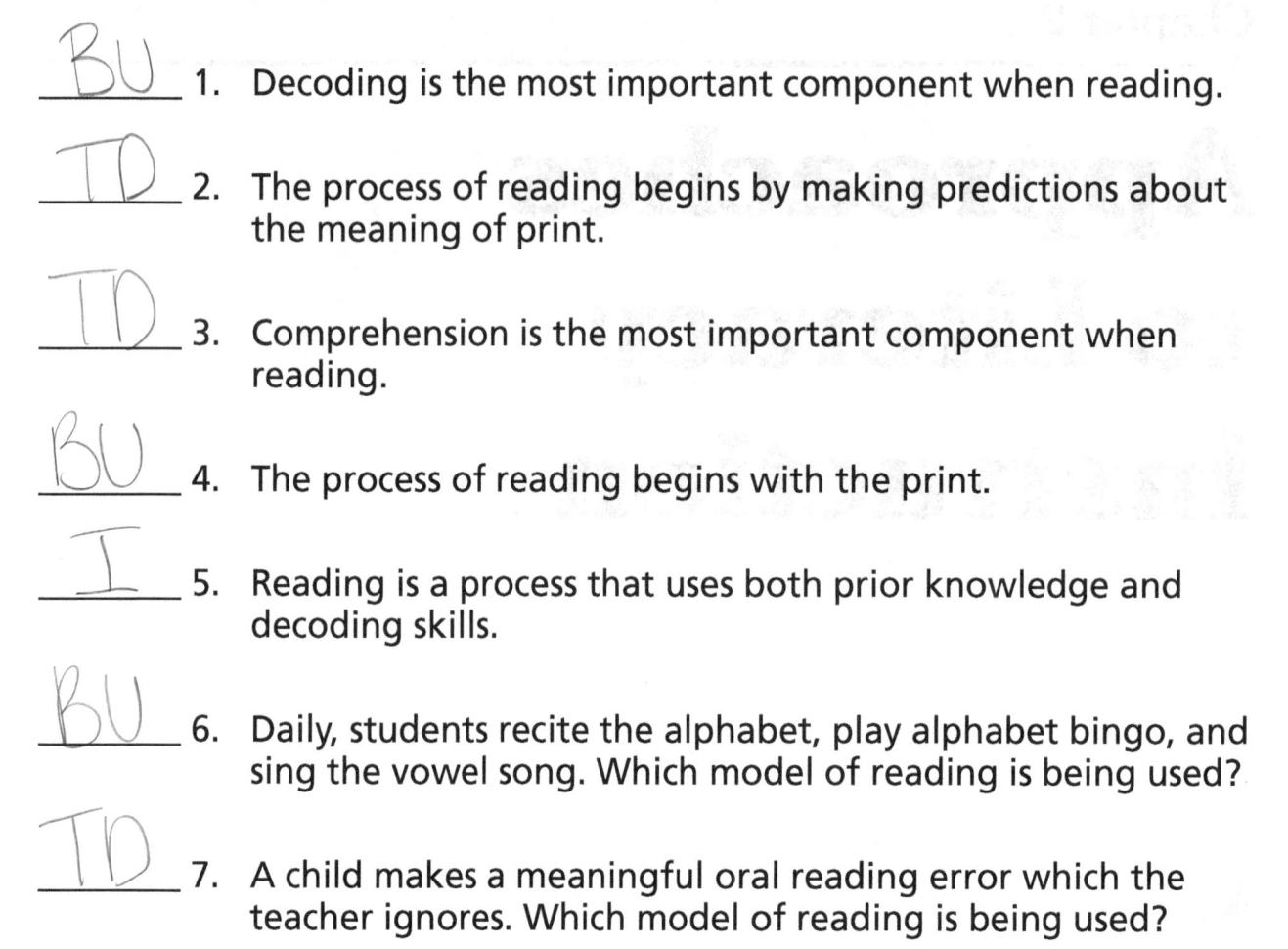

__BU__ 1. Decoding is the most important component when reading.

__TD__ 2. The process of reading begins by making predictions about the meaning of print.

__TD__ 3. Comprehension is the most important component when reading.

__BU__ 4. The process of reading begins with the print.

__I__ 5. Reading is a process that uses both prior knowledge and decoding skills.

__BU__ 6. Daily, students recite the alphabet, play alphabet bingo, and sing the vowel song. Which model of reading is being used?

__TD__ 7. A child makes a meaningful oral reading error which the teacher ignores. Which model of reading is being used?

Using Basals in the Reading Program

Pros	Cons
- options for reading (below-level, on-level, advanced) - guided approaches - encorporates other subject matter (science) - specific questions that correspond with each section of the story	

Language Experience

A CONCRETE WAY TO SHOW THE CONNECTION BETWEEN SPEECH AND WRITING

"What I can think about . . . . I can talk about,

What I can say . . . . I can write
(or someone can write it for me),

What I write . . . . I can read,

I can read what I write (and what other people write)."

> ****DISCUSSIONS ARE THEN FOLLOWED WITH STUDENT DEVELOPED STORY TEXTS.****

Russell G. Stauffer (1980). *The Language Experience Approach to the Teaching of Reading.* New York: Harper & Row, 1980.

Characteristices of Literature-Based Instruction

Trade Books

Reader Response

Read-Alouds

Sustained Silent Reading

Thematic Units

Classroom Libraries

Learning Environment

Skills and Strategies

Chapter 3
Early Literacy

Ready . . . Set . . . Role
Parents' role in early reading

Amy Wahl

Parents have an important role in helping their child during the early years (Simmons and Lawrence, 1981). Teachers need to remind all parents that their children are *ready* for informal learning experiences at birth, the environment must be *set* for learning to take place, and their *role* is an active one in early reading.

I have created a list of ABC ideas on early reading for teachers of young children to share with parents. Parents are the child's first teacher; thus it is essential for classroom teachers to provide them with practical ideas that can be implemented in the home. Parents do not need to focus on specific reading skills to perform their role as reading teachers, but they can provide informal learning experiences which can foster an interest in and love for reading.

ABCs of early reading for parents

Assortment of books

Have an assortment of picture books, ABC books, poetry books, nursery rhymes, and fairy tale collections within your child's reach throughout the entire house. Book ownership is important for promoting the reading habit.

Bookmaking

Assist your child in creating his/her own books. You can purchase blank books or create your own homemade ones. Your child can dictate stories to you and illustrate them. Help your child keep a diary or write special events on a calendar. Bookmaking helps the child to see talk being written down, and it is fun for children to read their own stories.

Cooking

Cooking is a daily activity in which you can include your child. S/he can help read the recipes, add the ingredients, recognize food names and name brands, and become familiar with abbreviations. Kitchen experiences provoke questions and enable your child to experiment with new words.

Discussions

Your child's vocabulary can be extended through participation in discussions with you and others. It is important to be a good listener and let your child know that what s/he says is important.

Errands

Taking your children on errands exposes them to the print in their world. You can read and point out signs for fast food restaurants, gas stations, movie theaters, and stores as you do your errands. Don't forget to read billboards, stop signs, license plates, and street signs. It is important for children to become aware of environmental print.

"Ready . . . Set . . . Role: Parent's Role in Early Reading." Amy Wahl (1988), *The Reading Teacher,* Vol. 42, Issue 3, 228–231. Copyright © 1988 by International Reading Association. Reproduced with permission of International Reading Association in the format Textbook via Copyright Clearance Center.

Free play

Play is the child's work, and it is through play that s/he learns about other people and their world. Encourage free play and provide your child with opportunities to interact with other children. You can provide props for playing house, hospital, grocery store, and office. Puppets are excellent props for retelling stories. Other good investments include a sand box, magnetic letters, blocks, and picture dominoes.

Grocery shopping

Your child can be an active participant in grocery shopping. Invite children to write and read grocery lists, sort coupons, read grocery ads, discover labels on the food packages, and read the signs in the grocery store. Grocery shopping experiences enable your child to see the importance of reading in an ordinary, everyday situation.

Habits

Habits are formed early in life. Help your children develop the library habit by taking them to the library regularly. Young children enjoy having their own library cards and being able to check out the books they select. The library offers a variety of media materials, story hours, and other programs.

Informal learning

Informal learning experiences can start during infancy. You can turn daily routines into hands-on, concrete experiences. These experiences can help prepare your child for the formal learning experiences at school.

Junk treasures

Your child can participate in opening the mail—opening junk mail can be a treat. You also can read letters and other mail to your child. Children can help pay bills, answer letters, and write letters to friends and relatives. Children enjoy sending and receiving mail. With your assistance, they can create birthday cards and write thank you notes for gifts.

Kidwatching

Yetta Goodman coined the term "kidwatching" to describe an important job of parents (Lamme, 1985). Kidwatching involves observing your child to become familiar with what s/he knows and doesn't know as well as what s/he can and cannot say (Lamme, 1985). You can learn a lot about your child through observing in different settings.

Lap technique

The lap technique of reading aloud to your child provides a sense of security as you hold the child close and share books. Booksharing can create a special bond as you learn about each other and the world of books. The lap technique can help your child associate reading with a pleasant, nonthreatening situation.

Magazines

A subscription to a children's magazine is a worthwhile investment. There are all-purpose magazines such as *The Electric Company Magazine* and *Cricket Magazine* or special topic magazines such as *Cobblestone* and *Ranger Rick*. Children enjoy receiving their very own magazines in the mail. (See list of children's magazines.)

Magazines for children

Cobblestone is a history magazine which publishes children's letters, drawings, and projects. It contains information on historical events, interviews, suggestions for historical books and places to visit, contests, history questions, plays, photos and illustrations, and short stories. Box 359, Farmingdale NY 11737.

Cricket Magazine has "something for everybuggy" including reprints by children's authors, short stories, poetry, art ideas, cricket cartoons, crossword puzzles, and children's poetry and art contests. Box 51144, Boulder CO 80321-1144.

The Electric Company Magazine, published by the Children's Television Workshop, introduces children to topics such as the weather through games, stories, questionnaires, activities, and reader contributions. 200 Watt Street, PO Box 2924, Boulder CO 80322.

The McGuffey Writer publishes short stories, essays, poems, and illustrations by students in grades K–12. The following themes are planned for the 1988–89 school year: "Everything and Anything—Whatever You Want to Write" (Fall), "Friendship" (Winter), and "City and Country: People, Places, and Things" (Spring). 400A McGuffey Hall, Miami University, Oxford OH 45056.

National Geographic World, published by the National Geographic Society, contains stories of people, places, and things worldwide and games, crafts, and photos. Department 00987, 17th and M Streets NW, Washington DC 20036.

Ranger Rick's Nature Magazine, geared toward the primary grades, includes wildlife photos, animal facts, adventure stories, readers' letters, games, and nature stories. 6925 Leesburg Pike, Vienna VA 22184-0001.

Nursery rhymes

It is fun to share the nursery rhymes from your own childhood with your children. It is through repetition that they will learn the nursery rhymes and begin to recite them on their own. You also can share your favorite songs and fingerplays.

Opportunities for booksharing

Booksharing opportunities should become part of the daily routine before your child's first birthday. It is helpful to establish a certain time for reading to your child each day, and no interruptions should disturb this valuable experience. Booksharing can develop a sense of curiosity and enthusiasm for books in just 15 minutes a day.

Patience

The parents' role in reading requires patience. You need to create a supportive environment and encourage your child to experiment with language. Including your child in errands, cooking experiences, and other daily routines requires time and energy, but the benefits are many. Be patient as your child learns about the world.

Questions

Children ask many questions about things new to them. Be sensitive to these questions and take the time to explain the answers. In booksharing, you can provide time for questions before and after the book is read. Remember to ask a variety of questions which require your child to think critically about the story, and try to avoid focusing on factual questions which test your child on the story content.

Read aloud sessions

Reading aloud to your child requires some practice, and you need to consider the atmosphere around you. There should be good lighting, minimal noise distractions, and comfortable seating. Choose books that relate to your child's experiences as well as those that introduce new people, places, and experiences. Read aloud sessions can involve more than reading a book and talking about it—you can extend them through extra activities, such as baking gingerbread cookies after reading a version of *The Gingerbread Man.*

Sensory experiences

Your child needs to become aware of the 5 senses. It is not difficult to provide stimulating sensory activities. An example is a walk in the woods where the child can touch trees, hear birds, smell flowers, and see the leaves.

Television time

You can help your children develop good television habits and help them monitor their TV time. You need to select worthwhile programs and watch and discuss them with your children. Discussions make TV time a less passive activity.

Unpressured learning

You do not need to put extra pressure on your children to read words, but you can encourage them to read their world as they experience it. Be understanding and supportive.

Value reading

Become a reading role model, Your child should see you getting into books, magazines, and newspapers. It is important for her/him to see the different purposes for reading, such as reading for information, pleasure, and survival in a world saturated with print. Reading should be valued in your home.

Writing experiences

Writing is an essential in the reading process. Writing materials like pens, pencils, crayons, markers, and an assortment of paper should be available for experimenting. You might even want to have a special writing spot. Writing experiences include letter writing, making labels for photo albums or other household items, journal writing, story writing, and making words for wordless picture books.

Resource list for parents

Buller, Dorothy, and Marie Clay. *Reading Begins at Home.* Exeter, NH: Heinemann, 1982.
Goodman, Ken. *what's Whole in Whole Language?* Portsmouth, NH: Heinemann, 1986.
Larrick, Nancy. *A Parent's Guide to Children's Reading.* New York, NY: Bantam Books, 1982.
Schickendanz, Judith A. *More Than ABCs: The Early Stages of Reading and Writing.* Washington, DC: National Association for the Education of Young Children, 1986 (1834 Connecticut Avenue NW, Washington DC 20009).
Taylor, Denny, and Dorothy Strickland. "Family Literacy: Myths and Magic." In *The Pursuit of Literacy,* edited by Michael Sampson. Dubuque, IA: Kendall/Hunt, 1986.
Trelease, Jim. *The Read-Aloud Handbook.* Fairfield, PA: Penguin Books, 1982.

eXtra attention

Your role in early reading requires you to devote extra attention to your children's needs and help with their first encounters with print. You can obtain help from books such as *The Read Aloud Handbook* (Trelease, 1982) and *A Parent's Guide to Children's Reading* (Larrick, 1982). (See list of resources for parents.)

Your literate home

Create a nurturing and literate environment for your young child to learn and grow in. The experiences in your home can make a difference in your child's reading' development.

Zoo trips

Zoo trips, museums, amusement parks, and community parks are places that you can visit with your child. Visits to these special places engage your child in new experiences to learn from and talk about. These experiences can be extended by using children's literature before and after the visits.

References

Lamme, Linda Leonard. *Growing Up Reading.* Washington, DC: Acropolis Books, 1985.

Simmons, Barbara, and Paula smith Lawrence. "Beginning Reading: Welcoming Parents," *Childhood Education,* vol. 57 (January–February 1981), pp. 156–59.

Compare and Contrast
Reading readiness and emergent literacy

Stages of Spelling Development

Scribbling

- Gross motor
- Controlled
- Letter

Precommunicative

Prephonemic

Phonemic

- Early
- Later

Transitional

Conventional

Phonetic Assessment

Determine at which spelling phase the child is writing.

1.

2.

I L M M

"I love my mom."

3.

OTSTdI SAW A LgtNiNg BAg. It WS yollo.

"Outside I saw a Lightning bug. It was yellow."

4.

Three is grater then one.

"Three is greater than one."

5.

⁀⁀⁀⁀⁀⁀⁀

"Daddy's name is Robert."

6.

I PLAY W
"I   play   with

MY SSTR I
my   sister.   I

LAK Hr
like   her."

7.

Emergent Reader Observation

1. Select three picture books that YOU enjoy and can be read aloud to a child in 15 minutes or less. You'll be bringing along three books to guarantee that you'll have at least one book to read to the child that he/she has never seen before.

2. To prepare, read the books several times so you are thoroughly familiar with them, rehearse the questions on the following page and decide which specific pages of the books you'll probably use for certain questions. Take books, questions, paper, and pencil with you to the observation.

3. When you first meet your child, introduce yourself. Perhaps tell him/her that you are a student, too. Explain that you'll be reading a book to him/her and will also be asking questions about the book. Make sure the child understands that it's OK if he/she doesn't know all the answers.

4. Lay all three books out in front of the child and ask him/her which book he/she has never seen or heard read aloud before. Use that book for your observation.

5. As you read with the child, keep the questions close by. Either take notes as you read or right after the child returns to the classroom. Try to record as exactly as possible the child's responses.

6. Make sure that you are reading in a quiet place, away from distractions.

7. There is no need to tell the child if he/she is answering correctly, and don't tell the child the answers. This tends to focus the child too much on correctness. Encourage him/her to try and applaud all efforts.

Reading Observation Write-Up

Briefly describe the child: first name only, age, sex, any handicapping condition, and other pertinent information.

By number, describe the child's responses to each question. Make your descriptions clear enough that I will be able to visualize the event. Draw interpretations if possible. For example, if the child was unable to identify a sentence, indicate what the child DID say and WHY you believe he/she said it.

Conclude with a summary paragraph that expresses your perceptions and reactions to this child's knowledge of print and its relationship to reading. Recommend, using your own knowledge and ideas gained thus far from class discussions and text reading, what types of things an adult familiar with that child might do to further encourage the child's literacy to emerge.

Emergent Literacy Observation Questions

1. Holding the book by its spine and letting it hang downward, hand it to the child and ask:

    Show me the front of the book.

    Turn to the page where I should start reading.

2. Once you've turned to the first page of the story, ask:

    Where should I begin to read? Please show me with your finger. And then which way should I go? Show me what I should read when I come to the end of a line. (Make sure you ask this question on a page with more than one line of print.)

3. Read the next few pages aloud and ask no questions. Note the child's attentiveness and interest.

4. Turn the page and ask (there must be an accompanying picture):

    What do you think this page will be about?

5. Read another page or two. Then ask:

    Can you show me a word? Can you show me another word?

    Frame a line of print with your fingers and ask:

    How many words are between my fingers?

6. Read a page and ask:

    Can you show me a sentence on this page?
    (Have the child "underline" the sentence using his/her finger.)

7. As you are reading another page, leave out a word in one of the sentences. Be sure to choose a sentence that provides lots of clues for the missing word. Ask:

   What do you think is the missing word?
   (You might want to do this a second time with a different sentence to make sure of the results.)

8. Finish reading the story. Note any spontaneous remarks the child might say at the end of or anywhere during the story.

9. After the story is read, ask:

   What was this story about? What happened in the story? Then what happened? How did it end?

10. Ask:

    What would be a good title (name) for this story?
    (Important: Don't tell the child the book's title at the beginning of this exercise!)

11. General Observations:

    Did the child appear to be eager to read with you?

    Was his/her interest sustained throughout the story?

    Did he/she make comments about the story as it was being read?

    Did he/she ask questions, comment on the illustrations, make predictions, etc.?

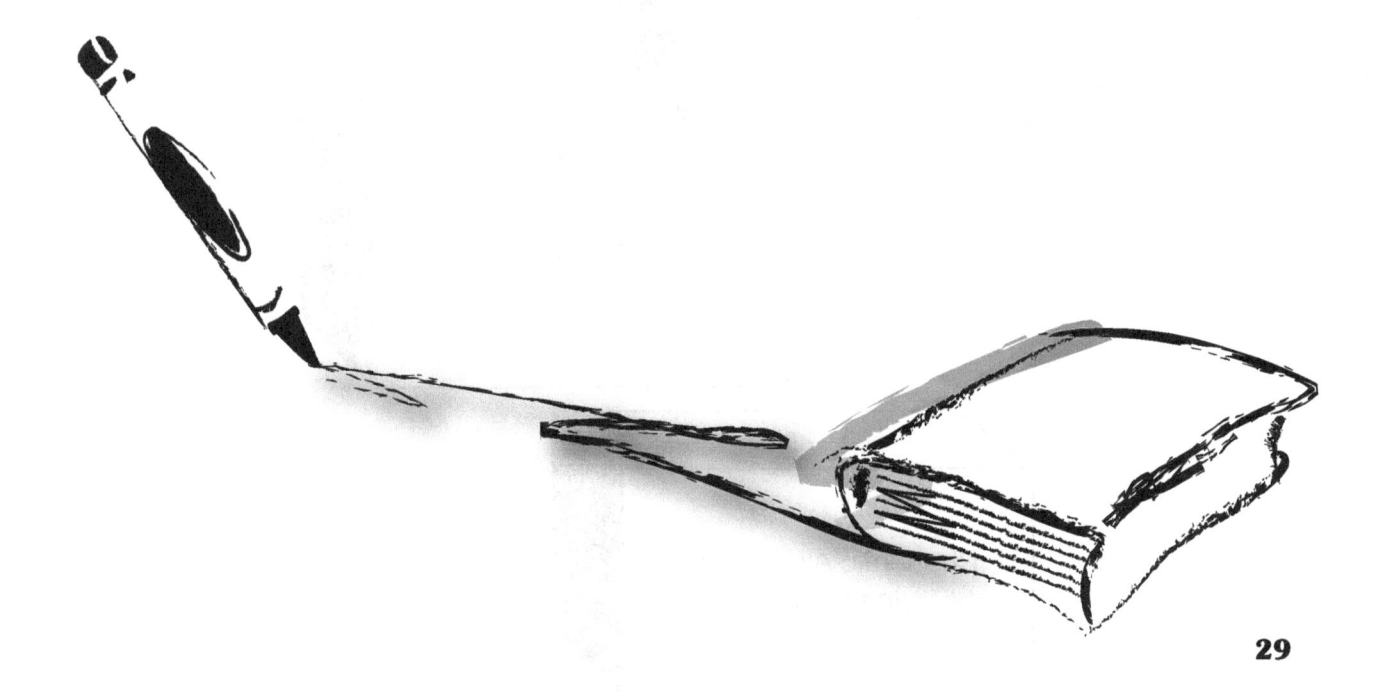

Chapter 4
Phonological Awareness

Put Reading First
The research building blocks for teaching children to read

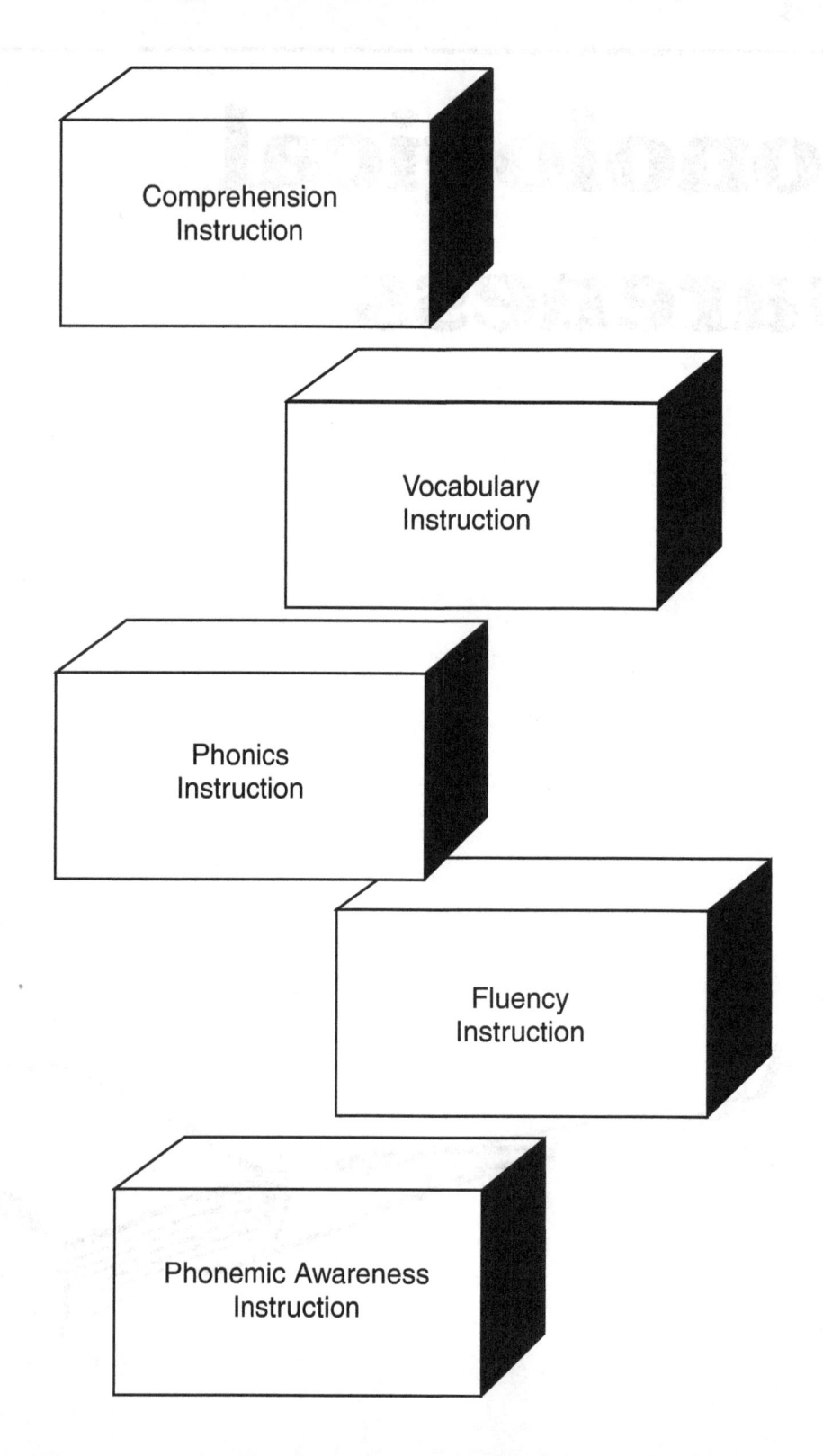

- Comprehension Instruction
- Vocabulary Instruction
- Phonics Instruction
- Fluency Instruction
- Phonemic Awareness Instruction

Phonological Awareness

When a child has achieved *phonological awareness,* he or she has the understanding that the speech stream—our spoken language—can be broken down into individual words, word parts, and sounds that can be manipulated. A *phoneme* is the smallest unit of speech. *Phonemic awareness,* then, involves being able to hear these small units of sound.

Phonological awareness → Think EARS (just sound)

Phonics → Think EARS + EYES (sound *and* print)

Yes, you can have phonological awareness without phonics, but you can't have phonics without phonological awareness.

Phonological Awareness Skill Sequence

Word Awareness

Mary / is/ a / little/ girl/ (five words)

Rhyme Awareness

- Rhyme recognition

- Rhyme completion

- Rhyme production

Syllable Awareness

- Blending
- Segmentation
- Deletion

Phonemic Awareness

- Isolation of beginning, medial, and ending sounds
- Blending
- Segmentation
- Deletion
- Manipulations

Developing Phonemic Awareness in Young Children Through Songs

Sound Matching Activities

(to be sung to the tune of "Jimmy Cracked Corn and I Don't Care")

Who has a /d/ word to share with us?
Who has a /d/ word to share with us?
Who has a /d/ word to share with us?
It must start with the /d/ sound!

(If a child responded with "dog," the class could sing the following):

Dog is a word that starts with /d/
Dog is a word that starts with /d/
Dog is a word that starts with /d/
Dog starts with the /d/ sound.

Sound Isolation Activities

(to be sung to the tune of "Old MacDonald Had a Farm")

Beginning:

What's the sound that starts these words:
Turtle, time, and teeth?
(wait for a response from the children)
/t/ is the sound that starts these words:
Turtle, time, and teeth.
With a /t/, /t/ here, and a /t/, /t/ there,
Here a /t/, there a /t/, everywhere a /t/, /t/.
/t/ is the sound that starts these words:
Turtle, time, and teeth!

What's the sound that starts these words:
Chicken, chin, and cheek?
(wait for a response)
/ch/ is the sound that starts these words:
Chicken, chin, and cheek.
With a /ch/, /ch/ here, and a /ch/, /ch/ there,
Here a /ch/, there a /ch/, everywhere a /ch/, /ch/.
/ch/ is the sound that starts these words:
Chicken, chin, and cheek!

What's the sound that starts these words:
Daddy, duck, and deep?
(wait for a response)
/d/ is the sound that starts these words:
Daddy, duck, and deep.
With a /d/, /d/ here, and a /d/, /d/ there,
Here a /d/, there a /d/, everywhere a /d/, /d/.
/d/ is the sound that starts these words:
Daddy, duck, and deep!
You all did great, so clap your hands!
(Clap, clap, clap, clap, clap)

Medial:

What's the sound in the middle of these words:
Leaf and deep and meat?
(wait for a response)
/ee/ is the sound in the middle of these words:
Leaf and deep and meat.
With an /ee/, /ee/ here, and an /ee/, /ee/ there,
Here an /ee/, there an /ee/, everywhere an /ee/, /ee/.
/ee/ is the sound in the middle of these words:
Leaf and deep and meat!

Final:

What's the sound at the ending of these words:

"Developing Phonetic Awareness in Young Children Through Songs." Hallie Kay Yopp (1992), *The Reading Teacher*, Vol. 45, Issue 9, 696–703. Copyright © 1992 by International Reading Association. Reproduced with permission of International Reading Association in the format Textbook via Copyright Clearance Center.

Duck and cake and beak?
(wait for a response)

/k/ is the sound at the end of these words:
Duck and cake and beak.
With a /k/, /k/ here, and a /k/, /k/ there,
Here a /k/, there a/k/, everywhere a /k/, /k/.
/k/ is the sound at the end of these words:
Duck and cake and beak!

Blending Activities

(to be sung to the tune of "If You're Happy and You Know It, Clap Your Hands")

If you think you know this word,
shout it out!
If you think you know this word,
shout it out!
If you think you know this word,
Then tell me what you've heard,
If you think you know this word,
shout it out!

(Teacher says a segmented word such as /k/-/a/-/t/, and children respond by saying the blended word.)

Sound Addition or Substitution Activities

(to be sung to the tune of Someone's in the Kitchen with Dinah from "I've Been Working on the Railroad")

I have a song that we can sing
I have a song that we can sing
I have a song that we can sing
It goes something like this:

Fe-Fi-Fiddly-i-o
Fe-Fi-Fiddly-i-o-o-o-o
Fe-Fi-Fiddly-i-ooooo
Now try it with the /z/ sound!

Ze-Zi-Ziddly-i-o
Ze-Zi-Ziddly-i-o-o-o-o
Ze-Zi-Ziddly-i-ooooo
Now try it with the /br/ sound!

Bre-Bri-Briddly-i-o
Bre-Bri-Briddly-i-o-o-o-o
Bre-Bri-Briddly-i-ooooo
Now try it with a /ch/ sound!

Che-Chi-Chiddly-i-o
Che-Chi-Chiddly-i-o-o-o-o
Che-Chi-Chiddly-i-ooooo
Che-Chi-Chiddly-i-o!

Segmentation Activities

(to be sung to the tune of "Twinkle, Twinkle, Little Star")

Listen, listen
To my word
Then tell me all the sounds you heard: race
(slowly)

/r/ is one sound
/a/ is two
/s/ is last in race
It's true.

Listen, listen
To my word
Then tell me all the sounds you heard: coat
(slowly)

/k/ is one sound
/o/ is two
/t/ is last in coat
It's true.

Thanks for listening to my words
And telling all the sounds you heard!

(The lyrics of "Twinkle, Twinkle Little Star" are structured to accommodate words with three phonemes, but they are easily adapted for words with only two sounds):

Listen, listen
To my word
Then tell me all the sounds you heard: g o
(slowly)

/g/ is one sound
/o/ is two
And that is all in g o
It's true.

Chapter 5

Word Identification

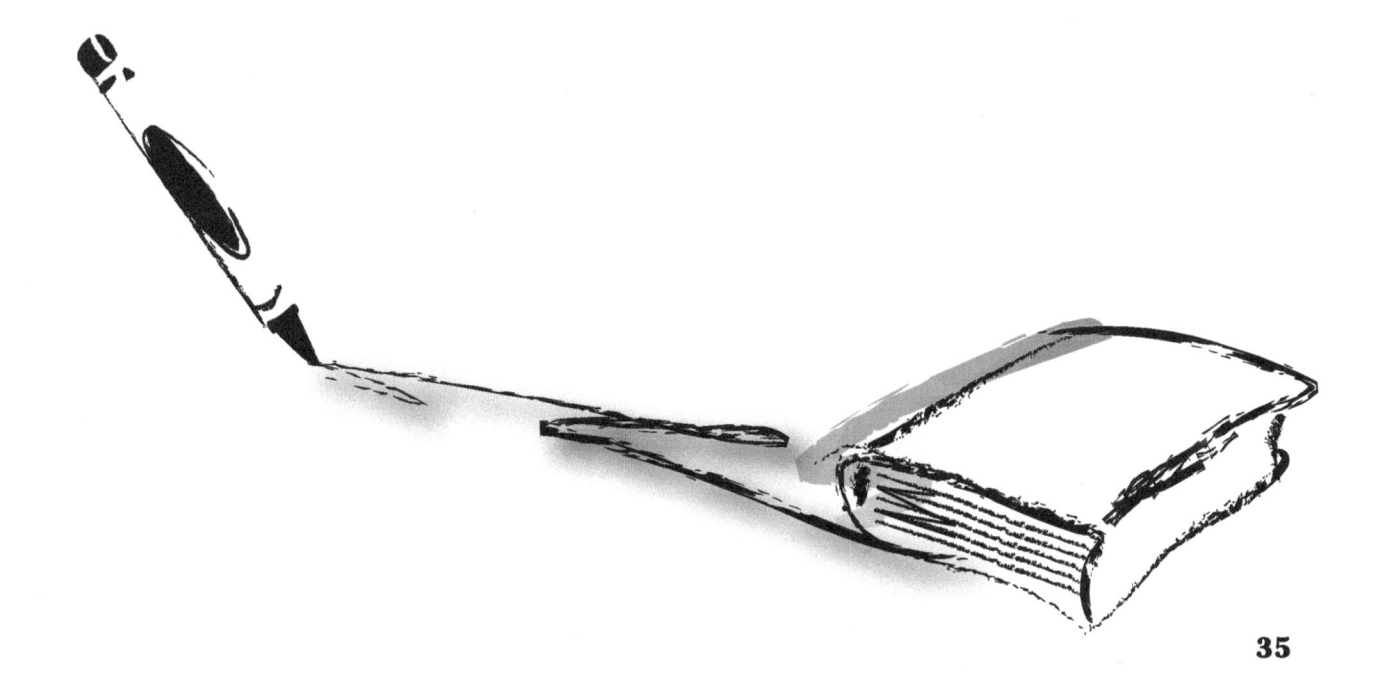

The Interactive Cueing System

Mary looked down the snowy hillside and saw a lake.

Three _____ . . . .

The Three Cueing Systems

    1. Syntactic cue

    2. Semantic/Schematic cue *(meaning)*

    3. Graphophonic cue

Three _____ _____ .

What Is the Student Using? What Is the Student Not Using?

Text: I gave the cat a saucer of milk.

Student: I gave the cat a cup of milk.

+ syntax, semantic cue

− graphophonic cue

Text: He slammed the door of the house.

Student: He slammed the door of the horse.

+ graphophonic cue, syntax

− semantic cue

Text: He ran down the stairs.

Student: He ran down the sars.

+ graphophonic

− syntax, semantic cue

Prompts to Help Children attend to Semantic, Syntactic, and Graphophonic Cues

Prompts for Semantic Cues:

- You said (child's attempt). Does that make sense?
- If someone said (child's attempt), would you know what he/she meant?

Prompts for Syntactic Cues:

- You said (child's attempt). Does that sound right?
- You said (child's attempt). Can we say it like that in our language?

Prompts for Graphophonic Cues:

- You said (child's attempt). Does that match the letters?
- If it were (child's attempt), what would it start with?
- If it were (child's attempt), what would it end with?
- Look at the first letter/s . . . the middle letter/s . . . the last letter. What could it be?

Sharon Taberski. *On Solid Ground.* Portsmouth: Heinemann, 2000.

Words That Should Be Taught as Sight Words

1. They appear frequently in print (high-frequency words)

   EX: the, <u>not</u> monkey

2. They have meaning in the reader's oral vocabulary

   EX: car and home, <u>not</u> turbine or abode

3. They cannot be pronounced by applying phonic generalizations (irregular)

   EX: one, said, some

A Phonics Test for Adults

1. The spi broak the coad and hiz leg at the saim time.

2. I hoap the braiv whight knite will sla the grene dragon.

---

1. scurt   plurk   burx

2. tawc   blawc   frowc

3. nonix   konix   fonix

4. cloon   floot   glooth

5. buzine   yazine   dezine

6. roat   praig   neaft

7. kwele   kwire   kwabe

8. wrast   gest   cest

9. browl   plowt   skowr

10. jimn   cymn   pumn

How Do We Teach Phonics?

1. Build on children's phonemic awareness and their knowledge of the way language works.

2. Integrate phonics into your total reading program. Use a whole-part-whole approach.

3. Focus on reading words, not learning rules.

4. Include the teaching of onsets and rimes. EX: in the word c a t, c is the onset and at is the rime.

5. Include invented spelling and the writing process in your program.

Contextual Analysis

Carl is so <u>pugnacious</u>. All he ever wants to do is fight. (context clue for meaning)

The tire went flat because it ran out of <u>air</u>. (context clue to decode)

Limitations of Using Context Clues

<u>Every autumn</u> the <u>foliage</u> changes color. (context clues work best where most of the words can be read)

I have a pretty _____. (not enough context)

Every <u>autumn</u> the leaves change color. (dependent on background knowledge and oral vocabulary)

The flag is _____ in the breeze.

Structural Analysis—"Chunking"

Prefixes (<u>re</u>read), suffixes (read<u>able</u>), inflectional endings (read<u>ing</u>), familiar syllables (h<u>abit</u>at), root words (un<u>read</u>able), and smaller words within the larger words (am<u>use</u>) can help readers decode challenging text.

Practice:

Flawlessly

Uncomfortable

Some Strategies for Figuring Out Words

- Look at the beginning letter(s). What sound do you hear?

- Look at the pictures. Do they help?

- Look through the word to the end. What sound do you hear in the middle? At the end?

- Think of what word would make sense, sound right, and match the letters.

- Start the sentence over, making your mouth ready to say the word.

- Skip the word, read to the end of the sentence, and then come back to the word. How does what you've read help you with the word?

- Listen to whether what you are reading makes sense and matches the letters (monitor). Correct it if it doesn't (self-correct).

- Look for spelling patterns you recognize.

- Look for smaller words within the word.

- Think of where you may have seen the word before.

Sharon Taberski. *On Solid Ground.* Portsmouth: Heinemann, 2000.

Chapter 5 Word Identification 45

Not sure what a word is?

S Sound out the word. Say it out loud.

C Check for clues in the sentence.

U Use main idea and picture clues.

B Break the word into parts, if possible.

A Ask another student for help.

Still aren't sure? Then

DIVE

into the *dictionary!*

Not sure how to read a word?

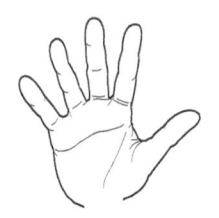

Five Finger Strategy

1. Say "Bleep".
   Reread!

2. Frame the word with your fingers.
   Reread!

3. Look for little words, endings, compound words, etc.
   Reread!

4. Sound out the word.
   Reread!

5. Ask for help.
   Reread!

Chapter 6

Fluency

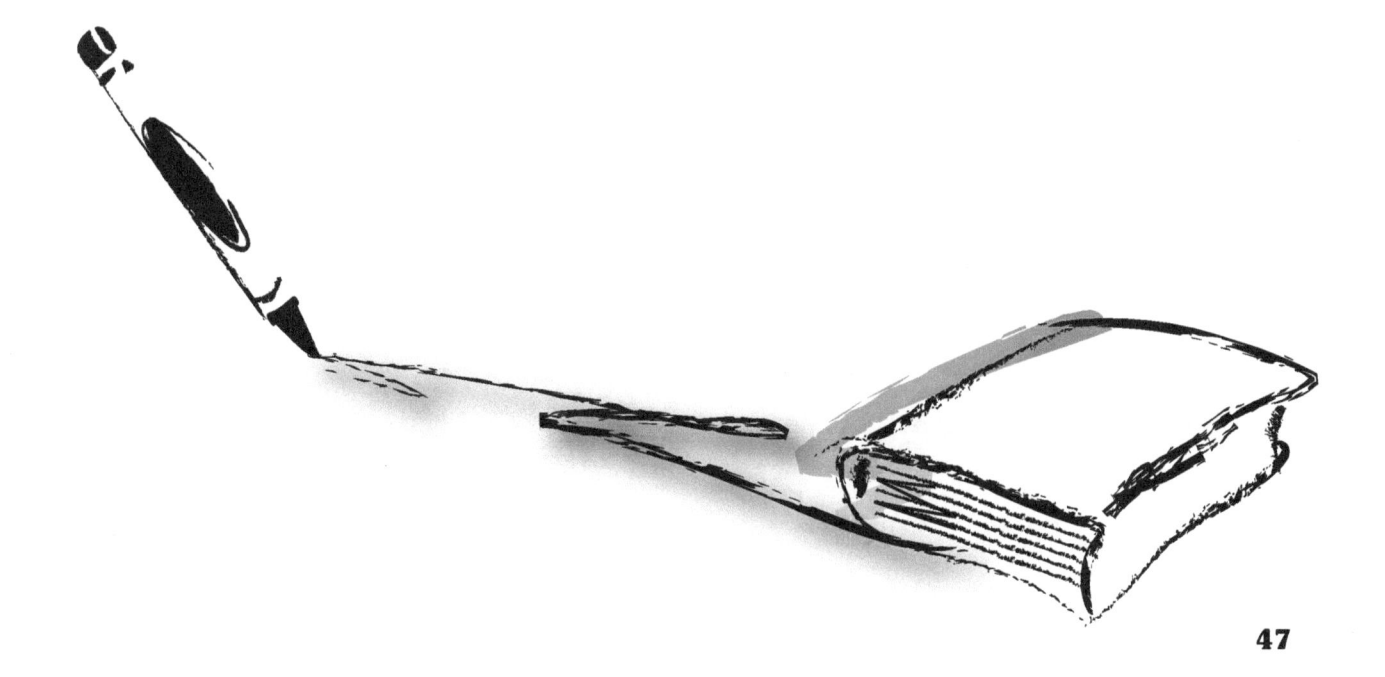

"Fluency" Anticipation/Reaction Guide

Before		After
T	*Fluency is the ability to read text quickly with expression. *(accuracy)*	F
F	*Fluency and automaticity are terms that can be used interchangeably.	F
T	*Research shows that children who reread aloud the same piece of text about four times, improve in both fluency and comprehension.	T
	*Fluency and comprehension go hand-in-hand.	T
T	*Silent, independent reading does not have a proven effect on improving reading fluency or comprehension.	T
T	*Readers' theater and choral reading are both research-based strategies to improve fluency.	T

What Is Fluency?

Reading fluency is a reader's ability to read material quickly, accurately, and with meaningful expression. (All of these elements together indicate reading fluency and contribute to improved reading comprehension.)

A fluent reader can . . .

1. Read at a rapid rate
   (pace—the speed at which oral or silent reading occurs)

2. Automatically recognize words
   (smoothness/accuracy—efficient decoding skills)

3. Phrase correctly
   (the ability to read a text orally using appropriate pitch, stress, and phrasing)

Fluency is important because . . .

It frees students to understand what they are reading.

Reading fluency can be developed . . .

By modeling fluent reading and having students engage in repeated oral reading.

Reading fluency can be assessed . . .

By using both informal and formal assessment measures.

Why Is It Important?

Recent research shows . . .

- In 2000, the National Reading Panel reported that fluency should be a key component of effective instruction.

- The National Literacy Council reviewed extensive research and found that effective reading instruction must include direct and ongoing instruction in five areas: Phonemic awareness, phonics, *READING FLUENCY,* vocabulary development, and text comprehension.

- Children who reread aloud the same piece of text about four times become better readers by improving their word recognition skills, speed, accuracy, fluency, and comprehension.

- Fluency and comprehension go hand-in-hand. Readers who are able to easily and effortlessly decode text, are better able to focus on the meaning of the text they are reading.

- Children who read fluently are able to cover more content area reading in a reasonable amount of time.

- Fluent readers feel more successful academically, and are more enthusiastic about reading activities.

- Providing instructional time for silent, independent reading DOES NOT have a proven effect on improving reading fluency or comprehension.

- Fluency is not automaticity. (The ability to instantly recognize a word) Automaticity is only one element of fluency.

- Helping students learn to read in phrases will improve their reading fluency and overall reading achievement.

Oral Reading Strategies to Promote Fluency

Radio Reading	*alternative to round robin reading *students perform preselected pieces of text *one student is the "radio announcer" *other students are listening to him/her as listeners of the radio
Shared Book Experience	*teacher reads text to students *students are invited to join in when they can *often used with a big book so students can see the text
Choral Reading	*groups of students orally read one text together *poetry is a good source to use *groups can be varied—boys/girls, sides of the room, soft to loud, etc.
Mentor Reading	*like partner reading *mentor can be a teacher, parent, older student, or even a classmate *two readers sit side-by-side *mentor provides support for the reader
Reader's Theater	*groups of students use their reading voices to perform a story or a script *performed in front of an audience *students read from a script (lines are not memorized)
Read Around	*students read their favorite sentences and/or paragraphs to each other *sharing favorite passages encourages fluent and meaningful reading
Poetry Club	*gives students an opportunity to choose, practice, and read a favorite poem to their classmates *poetry is meant to be read aloud!

M. F. Opitz and T.V. Rasinski. *Good-bye Round Robin: 25 Effective Oral Reading Strategies.* Portsmouth: Heinemann, 1998.

The Chocolate King

Hershey chocolates are so popular today//. But when Milton Hershey first became famous/ he was not at all successful/ in the candy business//. His first real failure/ was in Philadelphia//. Then/ he failed in Denver and Chicago//.

Milton Hershey continued to fail in some of the most important cities in the United States.//He finally decided to return to Lancaster/ Pennsylvania where he had lived as a child.//Mr. Hershey received some money,/ which made him change his mind about the candy business./ He began to sell candy from a pushcart/ along the streets of Lancaster./ This time / Mr. Hershey added caramels to his list of candies./ Suddenly/ his candy business was booming./ Milton made a million dollars.//

Adapted from Denenberg, D. and L. Roscoe. (2001). *Fifty American Heroes Every Kid Should Meet.* Millbrook Press: Brookfield, CT.

Rubric for Fluency Evaluation

1. Nonfluent Reading
    - Word-by-word reading.
    - Frequent pauses between words (poor phrasing).
    - Little recognition of syntax.
    - Little response to punctuation.
    - Some awkward word groupings.

2. Beginning Fluency
    - Frequent word-by-word reading.
    - Some two and three-word phrasing.
    - May reread for problem solving or to clarify (strategic reading).
    - Shows some awareness of syntax and punctuation.

3. Transitional Fluency
    - Combination of word-by-word reading and fluent phrase reading.
    - Some expressive phrasing.
    - Shows attention to punctuation and syntax.

4. Fluent Reading
    - Fluent reading with very few word-by-word interruptions.
    - Reads mostly in larger meaningful phrases.
    - Reads with expression.
    - Attends consistently to punctuation.
    - Rereads as necessary to clarify or problem-solve.

I. C. Fountas and G. S. Pinnell. *Guided Reading.* Portsmouth: Heinemann, 1996.

Chapter 7

Vocabulary and Concept Development

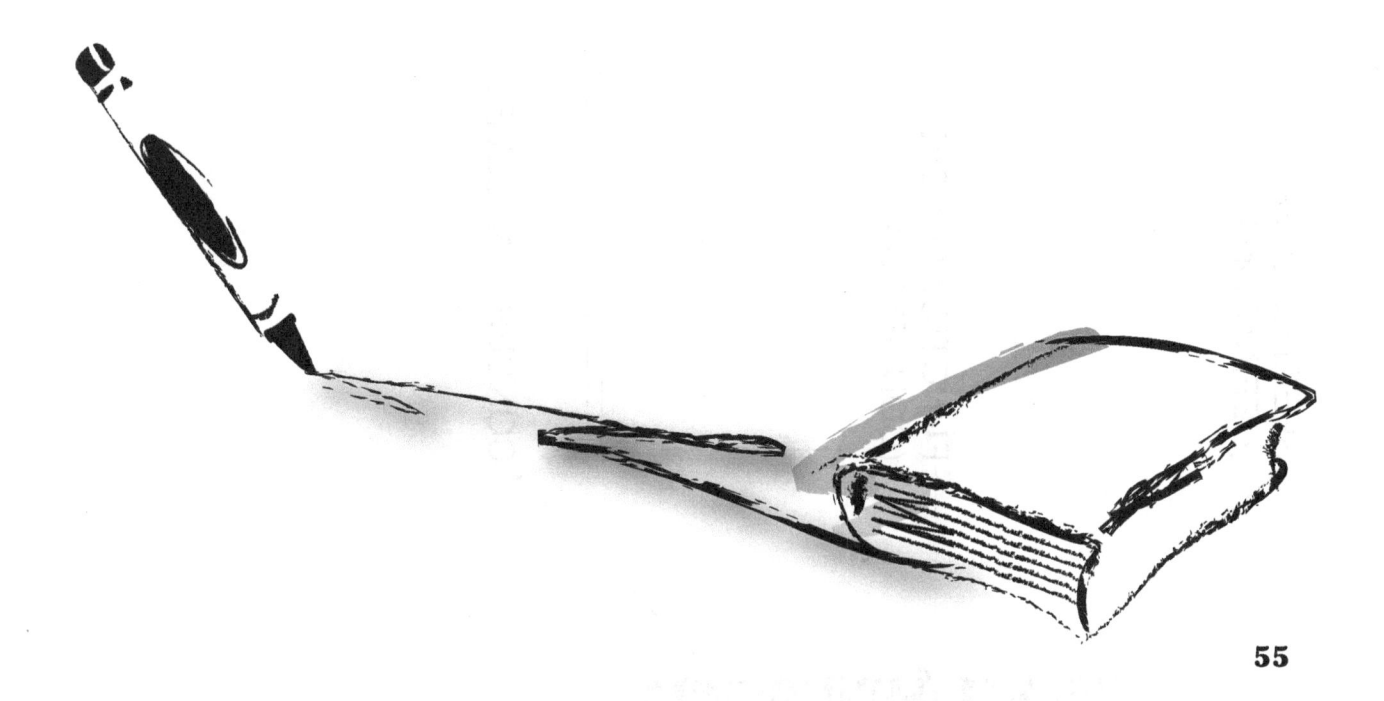

Vocabulary Levels

SPECIFIC LEVEL (DEFINITIONAL)

THE LEARNER HAS A WORD ASSOCIATED WITH A SINGLE IDEA, EVENT, OR OBJECT. (RECOGNITION LEVEL)

Example: "I HAVE A SCIENCE BOOK."

FUNCTIONAL LEVEL (CONTEXTUAL)

THE LEARNER UNDERSTANDS A MAJOR FUNCTION OR USE OF A WORD. S/HE KNOWS ONE APPROPRIATE CONDITION.

Example: "I CAN READ A BOOK TO FIND ANSWERS TO QUESTIONS."

CONCEPTUAL LEVEL

THE LEARNER UNDERSTANDS SEVERAL MEANINGS OR FUNCTIONS OF A WORD. S/HE RECOGNIZES THAT THESE MEANINGS ARE TIED TOGETHER BY SOME COMMON ELEMENT.

Example: "BOOKS ARE A MEANS OF COMMUNICATION."

Knowing a Word's Levels

Definitional Level

Contextual Level

Conceptual Level

Basic Guidelines for Vocabulary Instruction

1. Vocabulary activities engage the learner in the construction of word meanings from experiences, context, and reasoning.

2. Vocabulary activities enable the learner to recognize commonalities/differences between and among clusters of words.

3. Vocabulary instruction encourages the learner to generate predictive connections between words and the topic or structure of the selection—while emphasizing that words are not isolated elements, but rich semantic networks.

Vocabulary Instruction

Direct Instruction

1. Look at the word. Say it. "Vivacious"

2. Tell the meaning of the word.

3. Analyze the word structurally; relate it to other words.

4. Discuss the word. Personalize the word.

5. Students use the word in context or create their own definition.

6. Write it.

Some Indirect Instructional Strategies

- Word Map
- Semantic Feature Analysis
- 9 Squares
- Word Lines
- Word Sort
- Concept of Definition Map
- Rivet
- Concept Circle

Informal Strategies

- Language Games
- Word Play Center
- Etymology

Vocabulary Instruction

Direct Instruction

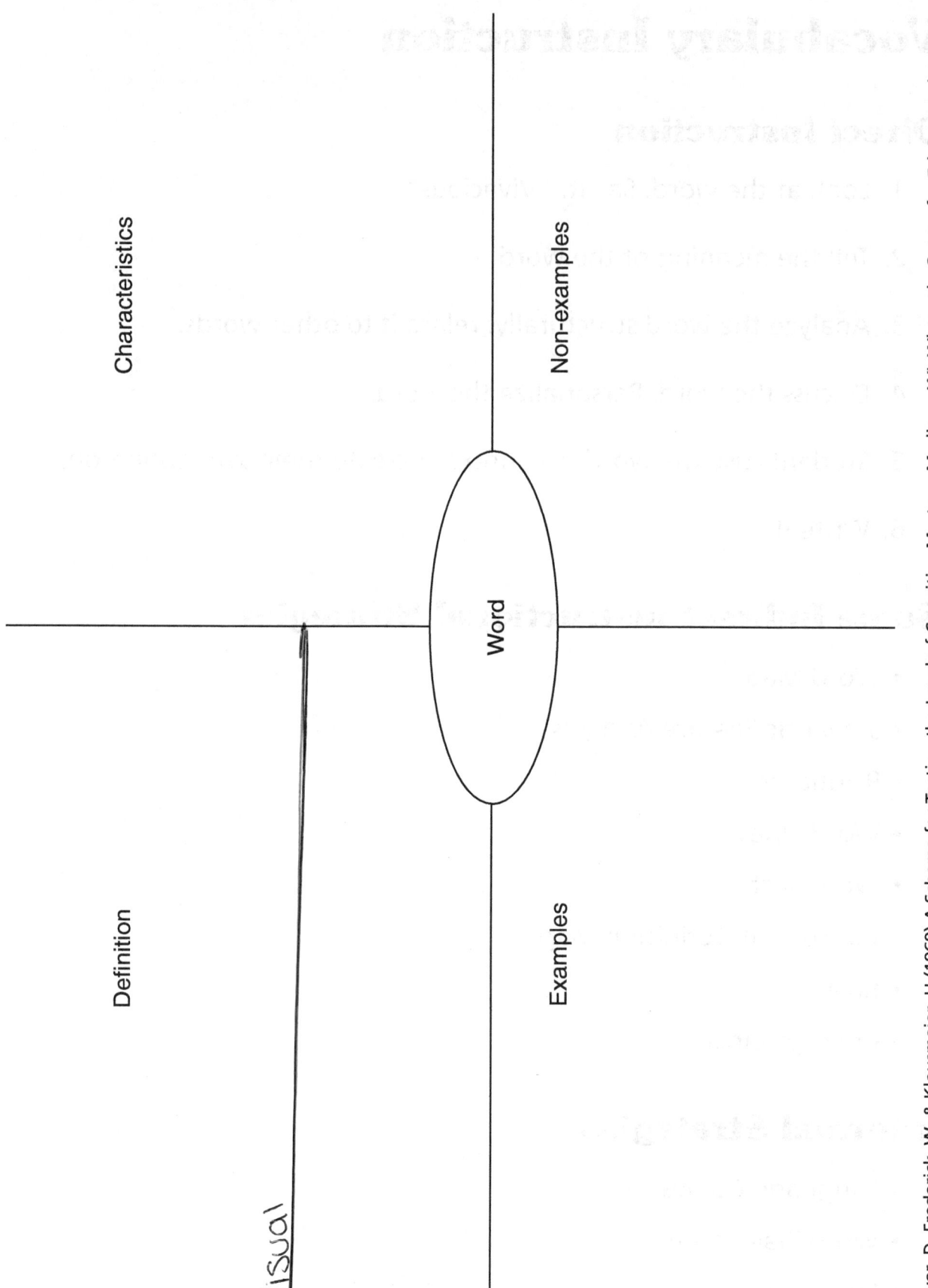

1. ~~Say~~ the word & use it in a ~~sentence~~
2. Define ~~the~~ number of ~~syllables~~
3. Analyze it & use ~~naturally~~ relate it to other words
...

Definition	Characteristics
Visual	
Examples	Non-examples

(Word)

Frayer, D, Frederick, W, & Klausmeier, H (1969) A Schema for Testing the Level of Cognitive Mastery. Madison, WI: Wisconsin Center for Ed. Research.

Word-Study Boxes

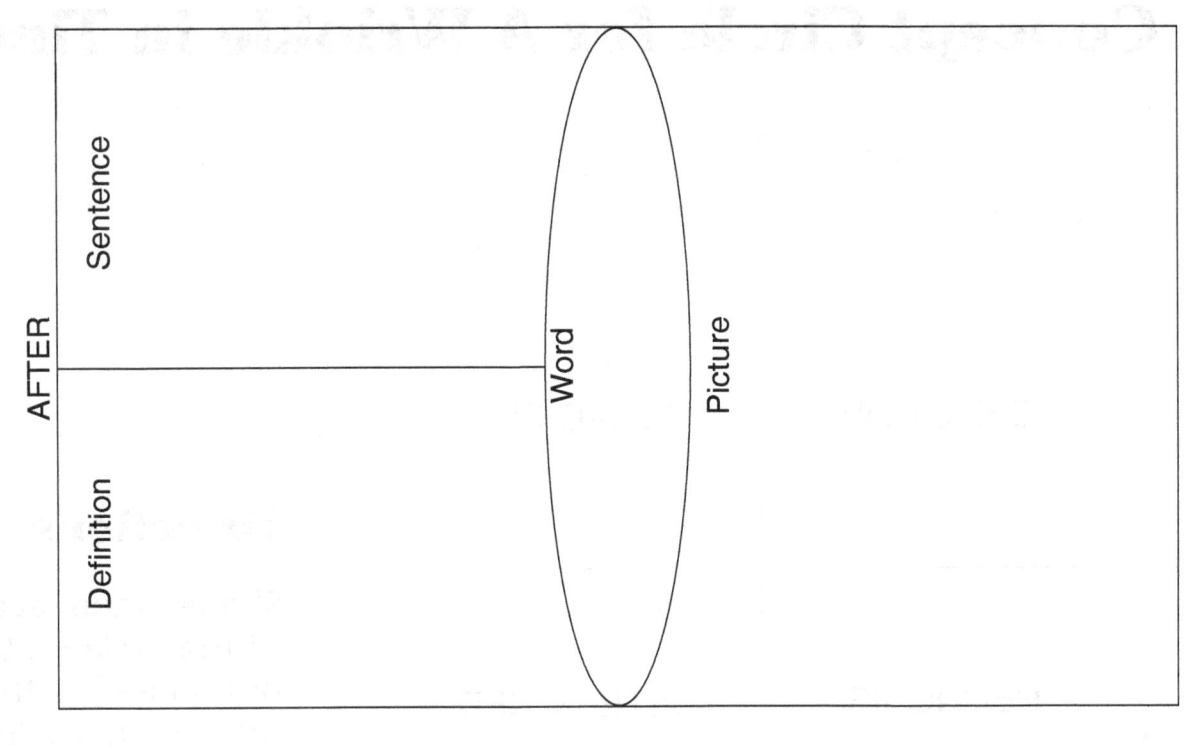

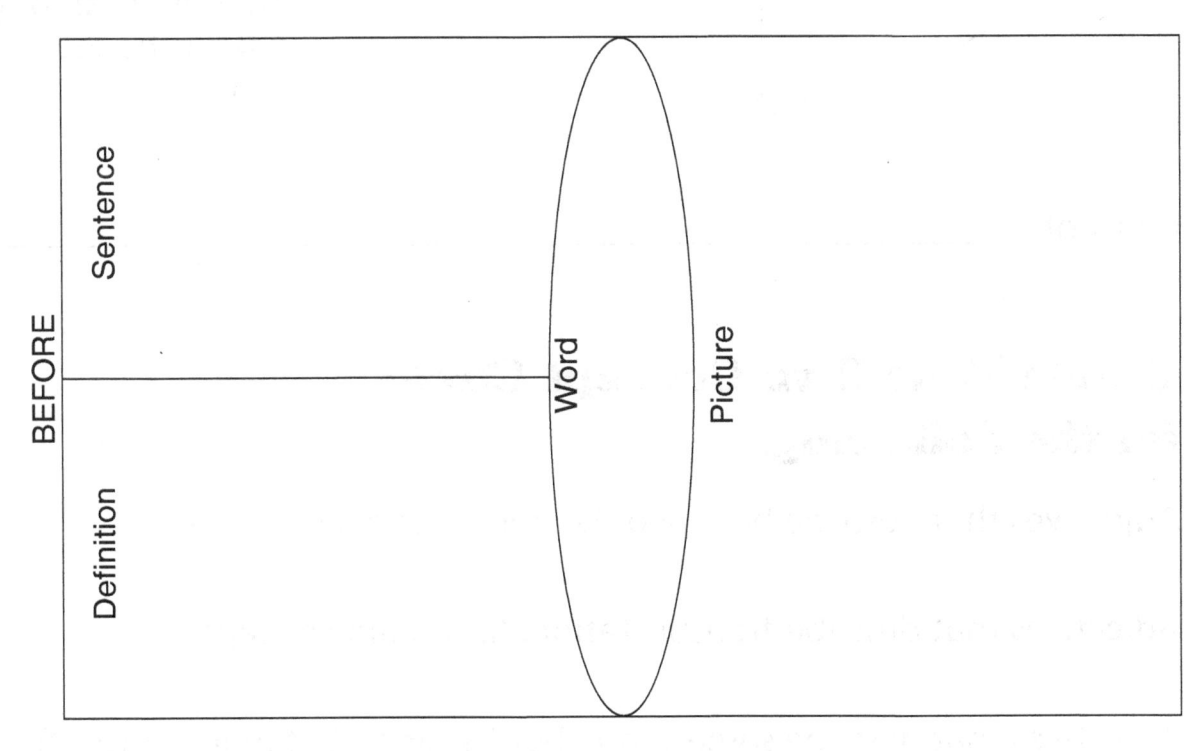

BEFORE

Definition	Sentence

Word

Picture

AFTER

Definition	Sentence

Word

Picture

Concept Circle for A Wrinkle in Time

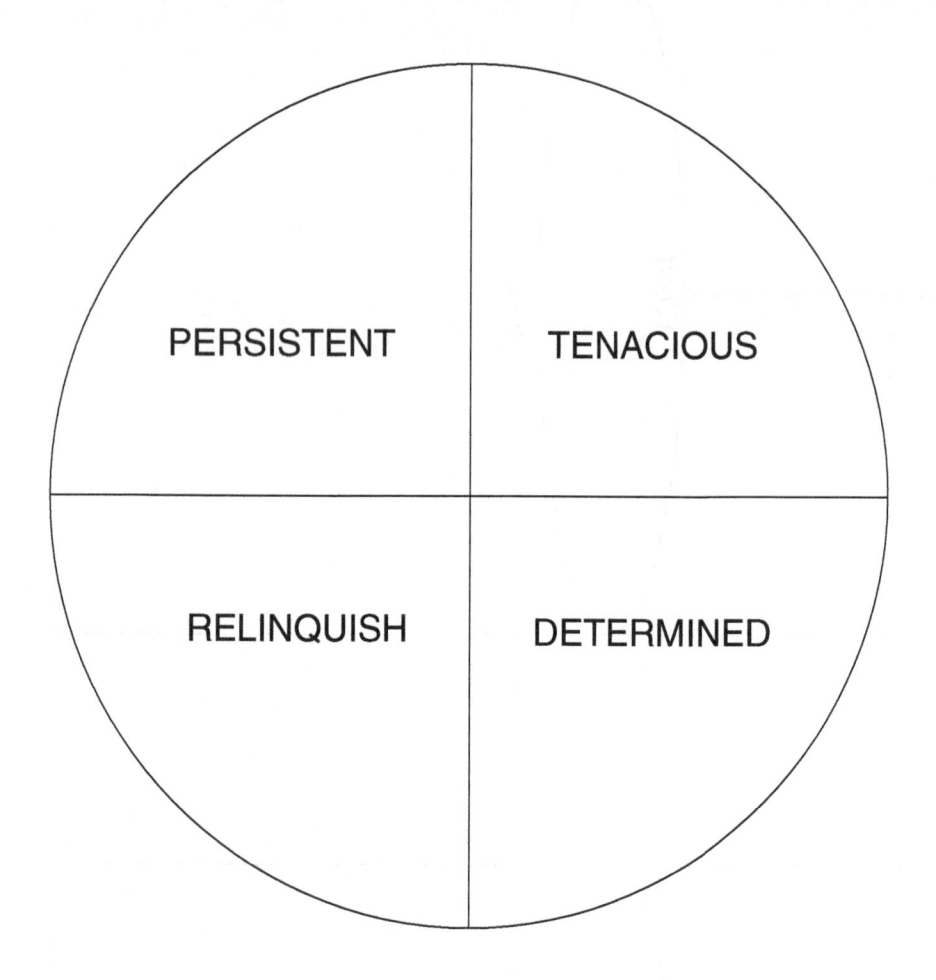

PERSISTENT	TENACIOUS
RELINQUISH	DETERMINED

Directions

Shade in the section of the circle that is not related to the other sections. In the space below describe the concept relationship that exists among the unshaded words.

Concept: _____

Create Your Own Concept Circle for the Following:

Adjectives that describe how people look. (List main concept)

Adjectives that describe transportation. (List main concept)

Adjectives that describe something about sports. (List main concept)

William Penn

___ ___ ___ ___ ___ ___

___ ___ ___ ___ ___ ___ ___ ___

___ ___ ___ ___

___ ___ ___ ___ ___ ___ ___

Rivet

Patricia Cunningham. *Phonics They Use: Words for Reading and Writing,* third edition. Allyn & Bacon, 2000.

Word Lines

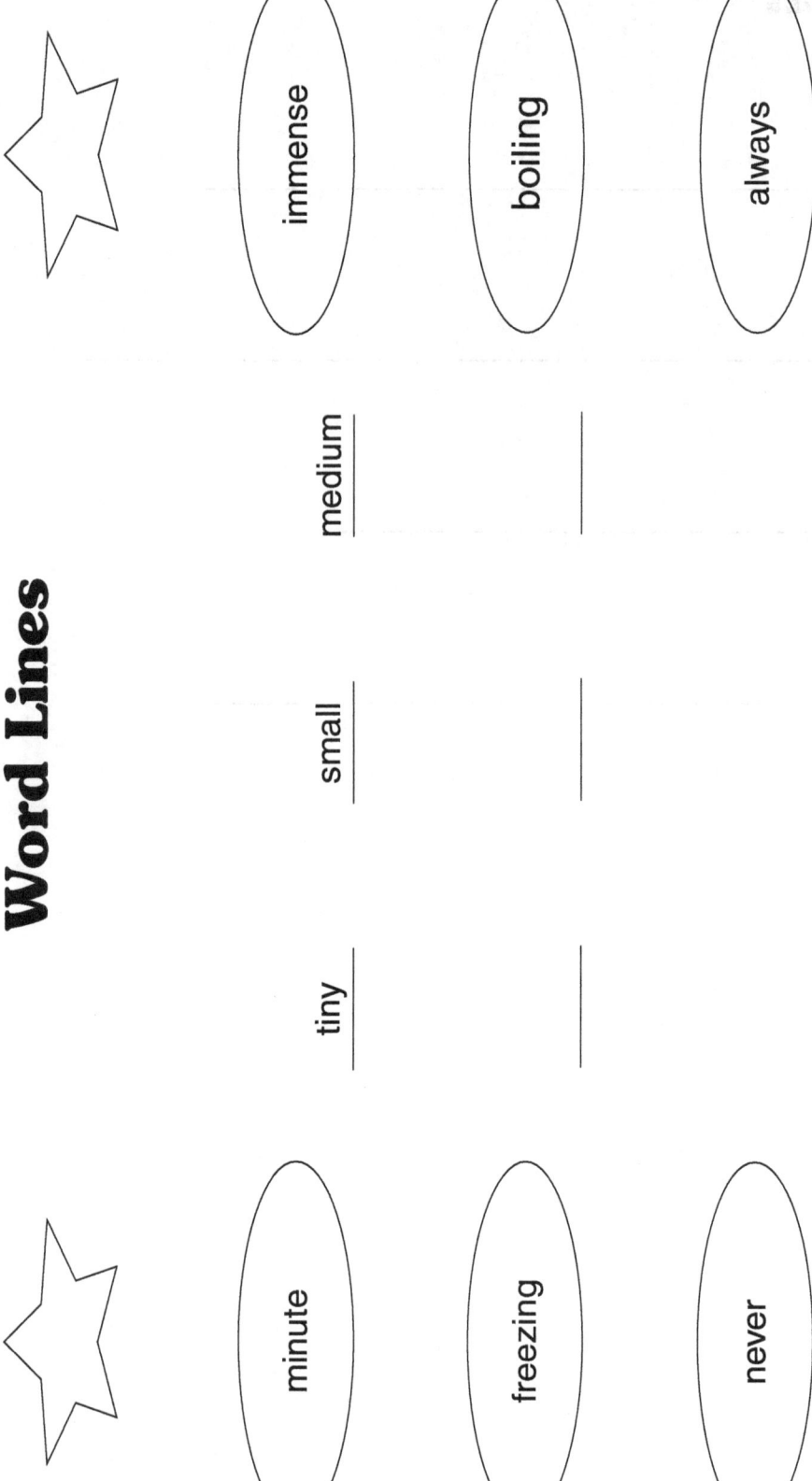

☆ minute _____ tiny _____ small _____ medium _____ immense ☆

freezing _____ _____ _____ _____ boiling

never _____ _____ _____ _____ always

Excerpted from Janet Allen. *Words, Words, Words, Words*. Stemhouse Publishing.

Semantic Feature Analysis Chart

	two wheels	four wheels	motor	passengers	enclosed
bicycle	+	−	−	+	−
motorcycle	+	−	+	+	−
car	−	+	+	+	+
skateboard	−	+	−	−	−

Context Clues

Linked Synonyms

Words with the same or nearly the same meaning as the unknown word. These synonyms are often found right within the sentence.

Appositives

A phrase used immediately after an unknown word to identify or further explain the meaning of the unrecognizable word. This phrase is usually found within the sentence.

Comparison/Contrast

The comparison or contrast of an unknown word with another familiar or known word. Key words to indicate that this pattern is being used are: "*rather* and *instead.*"

Cause and Effect

This pattern provides clues to the meaning of an unknown word and is often recognized through the use of such words as: "*therefore, since, after, because.*"

Use of Context Clues

Directions

Determine the meaning of the underlined word. What type of context clue was used to locate this meaning?

1. Because we knew he was not sincere, his <u>unctuous</u> manner annoyed us.

   Meaning: _____

   Context clue: _____

2. It is easier to take notes when an instructor sticks to the point and is not sidetracked by <u>peripheral</u> issues.

   Meaning:

   Context clue: _____

3. No science experiment was too <u>abstruse</u> for this man, since he had spent many years studying the subject.

   Meaning: _____

   Context clue: _____

4. The teacher said that the <u>diffident</u> child was much too shy to be in the class play.

   Meaning: _____

   Context clue: _____

5. The strange boy was not at all <u>sanguine</u> when he received the award, instead he was subdued and rather sad.

   Meaning: _____

   Context clue: _____

Chapter 8
Comprehension

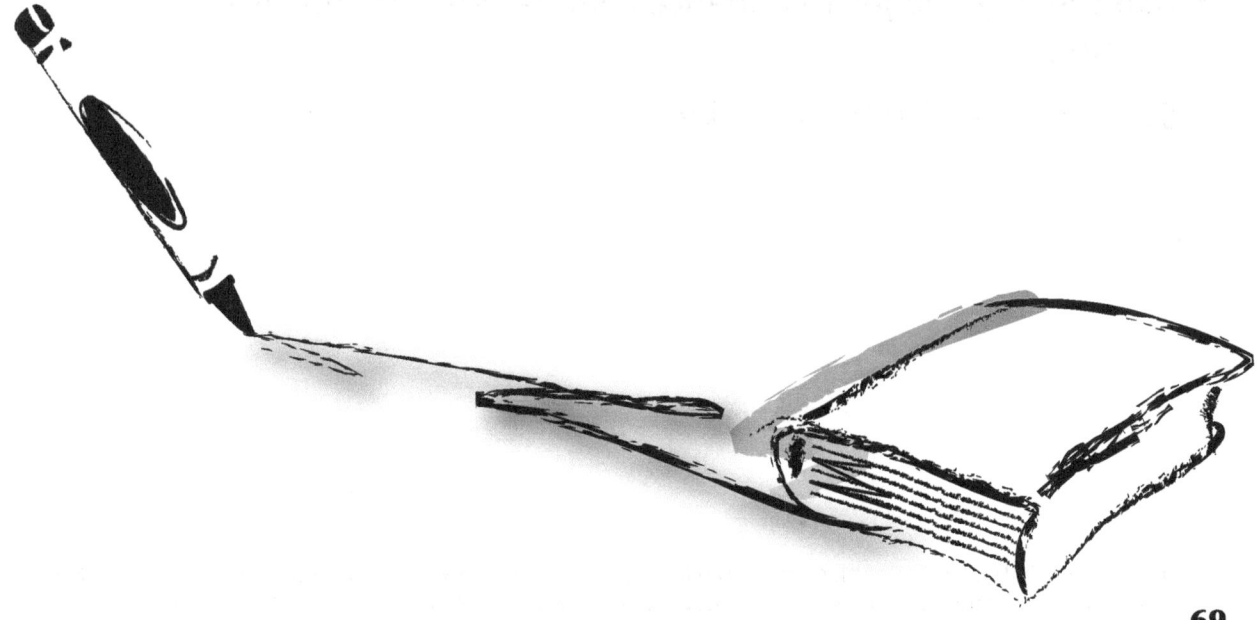

Comprehension Strategies used by Proficient Readers

A strategy is an intentional plan that is flexible and can be adapted to meet the demands of the situation.

Proficient Readers:

- **Activate background knowledge** and make connections between new and known information.

- **Question the text** in order to clarify ambiguity and deepen understanding.

- **Draw inferences** using background knowledge and clues from the text.

- **Determine importance** in order to distinguish details from main ideas.

- **Monitor comprehension** in order to make sure meaning is being constructed.

- **Reread and employ fix-up strategies** to repair confusion.

- **Use sensory images** to enhance comprehension and visualize the reading.

- **Synthesize** and extend thinking.

Janice Dole, Gerald Duffy, Laura Roehler, and P. David Pearson (Summer 1991). Moving from the Old to the New: Research on Reading Comprehension Instruction. *Review of Educational Research*, Vol. 61 #2, 239–264.

Alphabet Brainstorming about <u>Fairytales</u>

A nimals
B elle
C astle
D ragon
E lephant
F airies
G lass slippers
H appily ever after
I
J ester
K ingdom, Knight
L ove
M agic
N oble
O nce upon a time
P rinces
Q ueen
R apunzel
S tepmothers
T angled
U nicorn
V alor
W ishes
X
Y
Z

Princes — big ego, white, sexy, brave, tall, noble, royal, wealthy, charming

Reading aloud improves listening skills, builds vocabulary, aids reading comprehension, and has a positive impact on students' attitudes toward reading. It is the easiest component to incorporate into any language program at any grade level. Reading aloud is cost effective, requires little preparation, and results in few discipline problems.

—Regie Routman, *Invitations: Changing as Teachers and Learners K–12* (1991). McGraw-Hill.

Why Is Interactive Read Aloud so Powerful?

Read Aloud

- Exposes students to wide variety of literature in an enjoyable way.
- Builds content area background knowledge as well as general world knowledge.
- Helps students develop interests for later self-selection of reading material.
- Provides opportunities for assessing story development and characteristics.
- Facilitates students' abilities to compare and contrast by providing opportunities to look at commonalities among themes, texts, authors, characters, and conflicts.
- Fine-tunes students' observational/listening skills.
- Develops higher-level thinking skills.
- Offers opportunity to assess students' growth as listeners and thinkers.
- Allows students to anticipate or predict.
- Models effective reading behaviors.
- Offers time for students to practice cloze in a risk-free setting.
- Provides opportunity to assess reading strategies students already possess.
- Creates a way to assess interest/attention span and allows for increase over time.
- Provides opportunities to share a love of books with readers.
- Helps students develop a cohesive school program by connecting books to their academic and personal lives.
- Provides concrete models of writing for students as apprentice writers.
- Helps create a community of learners.
- Provides an opportunity to model respect for a range of reading and response.

Janet Allen (2000). *Yellow Brick Roads: Shared and Guided Paths to Independent Reading, K–12* Portland, Maine: Stenhouse.

Interactive Read-Aloud Lesson Format

Purpose Statement:

Vocabulary/Concepts:

Conversation Points:

p.____ teacher: _____
        _____

        student(s): _____
        _____

p.____ teacher: _____
        _____

        student(s): _____
        _____

p.____ teacher: _____
        _____

        student(s): _____
        _____

Deepening Understanding:

Further Questions:

The Man on Top of the World

Matthew Henson

To escape from a difficult childhood, Matthew Henson set out to sea when only twelve years old. By the age of twenty-one, he was an experienced world traveler. Then fate stepped in. While working in a store, Robert Peary, who was a famous explorer, stopped in. He needed things for his next trip. Matt was very helpful to Mr. Peary. The explorer liked Matt and invited him to go along on the trip.

From then on, Robert Peary and Matthew Henson explored together. Most of their trips were to the Arctic, in the cold North. Matt learned a lot from the Eskimos. Before long, he could drive a dog team. He could fix a sled, he could also build a camp in the snow. He hunted bears and seals and made clothes from their fur. Robert Peary said that he could not do anything without Matt.

If you like adventure and mystery, there are few stories that can match the experiences that Matt and Robert Peary had together. Constant danger, subfreezing temperatures, wild animals—it was all there. Only after three failed attempts did Robert Peary finally reach the North Pole. On April 6, 1909, after the end of a torturous thirty-six day journey, they were eventually able to reach their destination. They probably wouldn't have made it at all without the skill of Matthew Henson.

For many years, Matthew Henson's achievement was ignored in the history books because of his race. Robert Peary got most of the glory. People in the early 1900's just were not ready to cheer for a black man, no matter how big a hero he was. Eventually America has finally begun to appreciate Matthew Henson. In 1954 Matthew was finally recognized by President Eisenhower, who gave Matt a special medal for being an explorer and in 1997, Matthew Henson received a hero's burial in Arlington right next to his old friend Robert Peary.

Adapted from Denenberg, D. and L. Roscoe. (2001). *Fifty American Heroes Every Kid Should Meet*. Millbrook Press: Brookfield, CT.

Matthew Henson at the Top of the World

Making Connections to Text

Making Connections: Active readers make connections between what they read and their own experiences. Or they may connect a story's ideas with something else they have read or have heard about. Making these connections often makes reading more personal and enjoyable.

Think about each event in the selection. Then describe a similar situation that happened to you, to someone you know, or that you have read about or seen.

Event from Selection	Connection
1. Henson had a difficult childhood.	
2. Henson decides to become a sailor so he can travel and have adventures.	
3. Peary and Henson achieve their goal after many failed attempts.	
4. Henson is ignored due to his race.	
5. Henson's contributions to the expedition are not recognized for many years, but finally they are.	

What Is Think Aloud?

A THINK ALOUD is a teaching strategy that makes the <u>invisible</u> thinking process of reading <u>visible.</u> It is an attempt on the part of the teacher to model the thinking process that any good reader engages in when reading.

1. The teacher reads to the students while the students follow along with their own copy of the story.

2. It is best not to prepare a story ahead of time. Read as you do the first time. Of course, you will have to exaggerate some of the strategies.

3. Enjoy the story!

4. Use strategies, but don't identify them.

5. Just <u>think aloud</u> so the students will be able to <u>think along.</u>

Adapted by Roger Farr, Indiana University from the work of Davey, B. (1983). "Think Aloud: Modeling the Cognitive Processes of Reading Comprehension" in *The Journal of Reading*, vol. 27, 44–47.

Think Aloud Strategies

_____ Make a picture in your mind

_____ Predict from pictures and titles

_____ Ask yourself questions as you read

_____ Comment on ideas in the story

_____ Personalize the story for yourself

_____ Guess the meaning of a word from context

_____ Make inferences (predictions) as you read

Story Map

The setting/ main characters

Statement of the problem

Event 1

Event 2

Event 3

Event 4

Event 5

Event 6

Event 7

Statement of the solution

Story theme (What is this story *really* about?)

Values brought out in the story

Trio Reading

Definition: A cooperative learning strategy in which three students work together to practice and enhance their retelling and oral reading skills.

Procedure:

1) Group the children into triads. The makeup of the groups may vary according to needs.

2) Assign each student a role. One child is the Reader. The second student is the Reteller and the third child is the Checker.

3) Model the expectations of each role. The reader reads aloud with expression. The texts should be short enough that each youngster can have a turn performing each of of the three roles. The reteller summarizes the text after the reader has read. The checker reports to the group if the retelling was correct or not. The checker may give additional information if any critical facts are omitted by the reteller.

4) After the three youngsters perform their jobs, the students change places and roles and the general procedure is repeated. This activity is repeated again for the third sequence. Each child has performed each role.

Suggestions:

1) Set the chairs up in a triangle formation with the seats marked with the names of the roles: Reader, Reteller, and Checker.

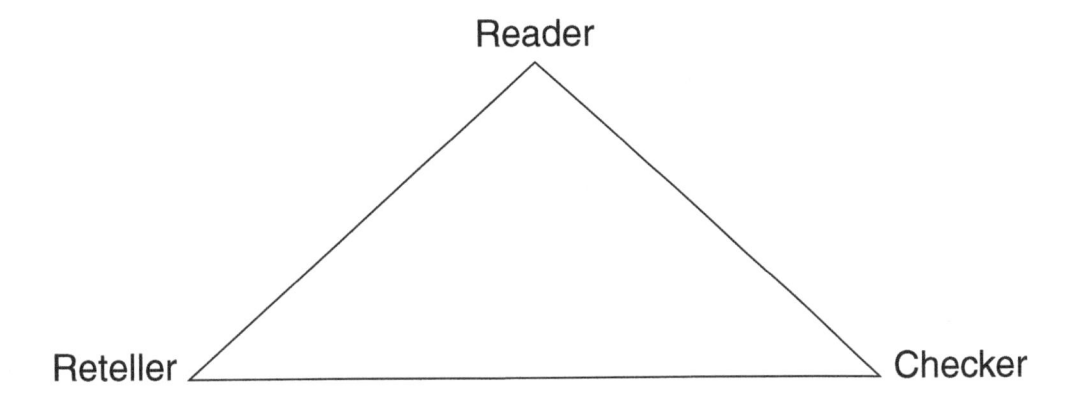

```
           Reader
           /\
          /  \
         /    \
        /      \
  Reteller ---- Checker
```

2) Have a chart listing the steps involved in the entire process for easy reference such as the following:

Trio Reading Chart

1. Sit together.
2. One reads, two listen.
3. One retells, two listen.
4. One checks, two listen.
5. Change seats and change jobs.
6. Use "Happy Talk."

3) Take time at the conclusion of the procedure to regroup the entire class and engage in a discussion about what they liked about the activity, what they did not like about it, and what they could do differently next time to make the experience even better. This debriefing is very important if cooperative activities are to run most effectively.

4) While the students are performing this activity, the teacher has a great opportunity to "kid watch" and assess how the children are doing in each of the different roles.

5) Compliment the students who are encouraging each other for using "Happy Talk" during Trio Reading. From time to time review with the class different ways of coaching each other.

Engaging with reading through interactive read-alouds

Shelby J. Barrentine

Interactive read-alouds encourage children to verbally interact with the text, peers, and teacher. This approach to reading aloud provides a means of engaging students as they construct meaning and explore the reading process.

Primary teachers have long used reading aloud as a way to introduce students to the plea-sures of reading and books, More recently, however, the purpose of reading aloud has expanded to include instructional purposes. For example, teachers read aloud to convey content in thematic units (Moss, 1995), to teach literature-based math lessons (Whitin & Wilde, 1992), and to demonstrate reading processes. (Harste, Woodward, & Burke, 1984: Holdaway, 1979).

Many teachers are dissatisfied with straight-through storybook readings that relegate listeners to a passive role. They seek suggestions to help them increase student involvement during read-alouds. The purpose of this article is twofold: to shed light on read-aloud events as rich literacy demonstrations that engage children through dialogue, and to share planning considerations to assist implementing interactive read-aloud events.

Approaches to read-aloud events

Although teachers differ in their specific read-aloud styles (Martinez & Teale, 1993), many limit the amount of dialogue during reading and then conclude the event with in-depth class discussions about the story. These after-reading discussions create opportunities for students to connect the story to their personal lives and for teachers to explore the connections that the students have made (Peterson & Eeds. 1990). After-reading discussions provide opportunity to "trace" ideas that were significant but unclear (Smith, 1990), to explore layers of meaning, or to develop knowledge about the elements of literature. These after-reading discussions are reflective and aim to deepen, broaden, and personalize story meaning.

Other teachers prefer to handle discussion differently. They read stories interactively. These teachers encourage children to interact verbally with the text, peer, and the teacher during book reading (Barrentine, 1993; Mason, Peterman, & Kerr, 1988). During interactive read-alouds, teachers pose questions throughout the reading that enhance meaning construction and also show *how* one makes sense of text. Students offer spontaneous comments as the story unfolds. They are also engaged with reading process information—how stories work, how to monitor one's comprehension, what to think about as a story unfolds. Thus, interactions about process are elicited along with aesthetic, personal responses to text. These interactions aim to engage children with strategies for composing meaning and to facilitate their ability to respond to stories. Interactive read-aloud lessons have been less thoroughly documented in the literature than after-reading discussions, so their potential for facilitating discoveries about literature and literacy is largely unexplored. While both types of read-alouds are valuable approaches, the interactive read-aloud approach is explored in this article.

"Engaging with Reading Through Interactive Read-Alouds." Shelby J. Barrentine (1996), *The Reading Teacher*, Vol. 50, Issue 1, 36–41. Copyright © 1996 by International Reading Association. Reproduced with permission of International Reading Association in the format Textbook via Copyright Clearance Center.

Conceptual foundations

Interactive read-alouds incorporate aspects of Cambourne's conditions of learning (1988) and of Goldenberg's instructional conversations (1992/1993). Observing how children interact and learn in everyday living situations, Cambourne developed a model that describes how children become proficient users of language. His theory of language learning asserts that certain conditions lie at the core of the effective teaching and learning in natural settings. These conditions are immersion, responsibility, use, approximations, demonstrations, feedback, expectations, and engagement. He argues that classroom teachers must simulate conditions available to learners in natural settings in order to achieve success in literacy teaching and learning (Mathie, 1995). Although each condition has implications for interactive storybook readings, demonstration and engagement especially support this approach to reading aloud.

A demonstration is a display of how something is done (Harste et al., 1984). For effective learning, Cambourne (1988) claims that a literacy demonstration for young children must emphasize how meaning is constructed, how language functions, and how language is used. He explains that demonstrations enable learners to select, interpret, and organize their developing literacy knowledge "into patterns and schemas that will eventually make them fully literate" (p. 47). Also emphasizing the role of demonstration in literacy learning, Harste et al. (1984) identify some of the information that is demonstrated to children during read-aloud events: how stories work, the relationship between page turning and moving through a story, how one reads, how one corrects (and monitors) reading/meaning, voice inflection and change, how language works, and what written language looks like.

They explain that the information available in a read-aloud is process and strategy information rather than just content information. Children can certainly gain new world knowledge from stories (e.g., canning is a special way of preserving food or butterflies experience metamorphosis), but relevant content knowledge is often gained in a single encounter. Unlike relevant content, process and strategy information is rarely acquired in a single encounter. As both Cambourne and Harste et al. point out, consistency and repeated demonstration are necessary to learn reading processes and strategies.

According to Cambourne, children do not learn from demonstration by passively absorbing information. To learn, children must become engaged with the demonstration. During interactive storybooks reading, engagement refers to the points at which the listeners have opportunity to respond personally and interpersonally with the story and with the process and strategy information used to make sense of the story. Engaged students interact with each other and the teacher in response to the text. With repeated engagement in demonstrations children internalize the ability to use process and strategy information.

Engagement cannot be forced, but it can be enticed. One way to entice learner engagement is to implement instructional conversations, which are a "particular kind of lesson [that is] geared toward creating richly textured opportunities for students' conceptual and linguistic development" (Goldenberg, 1992/ 1993, p. 317). These lessons focus on developing conceptual information, but the nature of the talk is conversational. Goldenberg states,

> On the one hand, they are instructional in intent, that is they are designed to promote learning. . . . On the other hand, [instructional conversations] are conversational in quality—they appear to be natural and spontaneous interactions, free form didactic characteristics normally associated with formal teaching. (p. 319)

Interactive storybook readings are similar to instructional conversations in that they aim to engage students in learning information—learning process and strategy information through seemingly unplanned, natural interactions with stories, peers, and the teacher. They differ from instructional conversations in that the conversation is ongoing during storybook reading rather than conducted after reading. The instruction and conversation are woven in with the reading aloud of the text. The following description of a first-grade read-aloud illustrates this concept.

An interactive read-aloud event

The first graders in Mrs. Herbert's classroom were engaged with the stories she read interactively. The interactions that follow are drawn from an event in which Mrs. Herbert read *Blueberries for Sal* (McCloskey, 1948). In this classic picture storybook, a human mother and daughter and a bear mother and cub go picking berries on Blueberry Hill. Sal becomes separated from her mother, and she meets and follows mother bear. In parallel fashion, the cub separates from his mother and follows Sal's mother. Eventually youngsters and parents safely reunite.

Opening up the conversation

Mrs. Herbert gathered the children to sit comfortably on the carpet and encouraged them to sit so they could see the book. She held the book in a position that kept the print and illustrations in view of the students. She reminded them that over the past few days they had been talking, reading, and writing about bears. Next she explained that the new story, also about bears, was titled *Blueberries for Sal.* As she prepared students for listening to the story, Mrs. Herbert displayed the illustrated endpaper and asked them to identify the two main (human) characters, invited them to make predictions about the setting, and mentioned the name of the author/illustrator.

T: Let's preview the pictures here. Who do you think this might be? [She displays the endpaper and points to Sal's mother who is in the kitchen pouring blueberries into a canning jar.]

S1: They're gonna make berry pie!

S2: The mama.

T: And who might this be?

S3: The—the—Sal!

T: Very good. Do you think they live in the city or the country?

Students: (overlapping comments). Country.City. They might be both.

T: Country? What makes you think they live in the country?

S: 'Cause there's a lot of trees.

T: A lot of trees. Okay. Do you see any big, tall buildings and skyscrapers like we've talked about in our social studies book?

Students: No.

S: They live in the country.

S: They live in the forest.

T: Here's the title page, *Blueberries for Sal.* This is by Robert McCloskey. He's written some other storied that we have read. Raise your hand if you've heard *Make Way for Ducklings*.

Already important literacy demonstrations were taking place: Readers remembered other titles by the same author, readers examined various pages of a book before reading the story, readers used illustrations to make predictions. The kitchen window in the illustration looks out over a rural scene, and the teacher demonstrated to the students that they could use the illustration to make predictions about the story. The overlapping comments indicated that looking at the window scene did not establish the setting for some students. Mrs. Herbert focused on the "country" response and had a student justify it. Further, she engaged them by activating their common knowledge gained from their social studies lessons to help them confirm that the story would take place in the country rather than in the city. It was important that Mrs. Herbert began the read-aloud with this comfortable exchange of information in which many children were verbally involved, setting the conversational atmosphere that lasted throughout the event.

Ongoing interaction

Throughout the read-aloud the teacher can maintain a conversational tone by inviting brief interactions. Ongoing interactions help students notice aspects of the story that they might otherwise overlook, develop an informed perspective on a character, or consider each other's ideas. Note for example in the following interaction that Mrs. Herbert invited students to consider Sal's feelings as she sits in a patch of berries and eats them.

T: How do you think Sal's feeling right now? Carley?

Carley: Happy.

T: You think she's feeling happy?

Carley: Because there is a smile on her face.

T: Do you think she likes blueberries?

Students: Yes!

T: What makes you think she likes blueberries?

S: Because she is eating them right away.

T: She's popping them right into her mouth, isn't she?

Through dialogue, an informed perspective on this character, Sal, was constructed by all participants in the setting. Students heard each other's ideas, and those who had not reflected on Sal's mood now had an opportunity to do so. Listeners had more to think about—more to notice—as the story progressed. Rather than connecting with Sal's feelings only once, later the teacher engaged the class in articulating what they had noticed about Sal's feelings.

Response and balancing talk and text

Children have many responses to stories, and during interactive reading they have opportunity to bring their responses into the social realm. For example, during this story event when the students realized that Sal has separated from her mother, some students began to chatter among themselves, and several raised their hands to share. The teacher asked one student to relay a personal experience.

S: One time we were in the market and my mom thought I was right behind her. So she went to another spot and then I couldn't see her. And I looked down on two aisles and started crying. Then I caught up with her.

T: How do you feel when that happens?

S: Sad.

T: Everybody, how do you feel?

Students: Sad.

T: And scared, too?

Students: Yeah.

One possible criticism of interactive read-alouds is that too much dialogue during reading could interfere with aesthetic aspects of good literature. Overanalysis of characters, too much informing, repeatedly activating background knowledge, and even lengthy sharing of personal experiences may disrupt the flow of the story and, thus, disrupt the pleasure of hearing the story read aloud. Harker (1988) found that when talk during read-alouds shifts away from the story itself, comprehension is reduced. But drawing upon students' personal experiences builds story relevance. In the above interaction, Mrs. Herbert used one student's experience to have all students connect their individual experiences and feelings with Sal's experience and feelings. Still, however the teacher faced a decision: Do I have all of the children share their experiences or do I move ahead with the story?

Providing opportunity for individual response and maintaining the balance between talk and text during interaction real-rounds require good teacher judgement. As teachers gain experience with reading interactively, natural sensibilities develop and indicate when dialogue is becoming too extended and out of balance with generating pleasure from reading a story. Lengthy interactions have enlarged possibilities for sharing, promoting, and extending student response to text, but extended talk is usually most appropriately saved for after-reading discussion.

Engaging with strategy demonstrations

Because read alouds are rich opportunities for literacy demonstrations, teachers can direct student responses when teachable moments arise. Teachable moments are opportunities for providing children with insights about process or content knowledge (McGee, 1995). During this read-aloud, Mrs. Herbert asked a timely question that engaged the class with creating an ongoing comparison between Sal and Little Bear. Collectively they constructed a sophisticated understanding of the parallels between the two characters. The construction was a demonstration of how to use the author's text structure to comprehend the story. Notice in the following interaction that, even though the teacher initiated the comparison, she provided meaning space for the students. For example, the statement, "They are both brown," was accepted even though there was no indication in the story or illustrations that Sal's skin color was brown. Also, the teacher did not clarify when there was lack of agreement among the students about whether or not both Sal and Little Bear were "girls."

T: Can you think of a way that Little Sal and Little Bear are alike? Bart?

Bart: They're both little.

T: They're both little. Yes, they are. Matt, what do you think?

Matt: They're both brown.

T: Okay. Um, somebody in the back, Ben. Do you want to look at the picture, Ben? Here's Little Sal, and there's Little Bear.

Ben: They're both girls.

T: Okay. Maybe so.

S: Uh, uh! It says *his* mother (referring to the text on page 18 where, indeed, the author refers to Little Bear with the masculine pronoun *his*).

T: Bart?

Bart: They both like blueberries.

As Mrs. Herbert continued to read, children interrupted the story to notice other parallels between Sal and Little Bear: They both stopped to pick berries, they both "had to hustle along to catch up" with their mothers, they both sat down in the middle of the bushes to eat berries. To sum up the parallels, a student commented, "It's the same, again!" And, another student chimed in saying, "They're doing the same thing. They're doing the same thing!"

To adults and some of the young listeners, the parallels may be obvious. To other young listeners, the parallels are an exciting discovery and subtle demonstration of how stories work. Using structure to make sense of a story is an important reading comprehension strategy (Dole, Duffy, Roehler, & Pearson, 1991). An advantage of weaving interactions into the read-aloud is that the discoveries are made along the way as a group. No one is left out of appreciating the clever way the story works. Moreover, everyone can make and confirm predictions since they are aware of the ongoing parallels.

Later, near the end of the story, a student raised his hand.

Ben: There's a pattern.

T: What pattern do you see?

Ben (pausing for several seconds before stating his idea): The bear and the mom do the same thing.

T: The bear mom and Sal's mom do the same thing. Yes. Good for you, Ben. There are a lot of good patterns in this story.

Ben carried his observation of the parallel pattern beyond the similarities between Sal and Little Bear. He observed that the mothers also "do the same thing." The discovery of these parallels assisted the students to develop a systemic rather than idiosyncratic understanding of the story. In interactive storybook readings, students are involved in an event that promotes involvement with stories and that demonstrates important reading process and strategy information. The teacher supports engagement by promoting conversational, nonartificial interactions that focus on the story and on process and strategy information—information that is naturally embedded in any good book. Through repeated demonstrations and engagement, children internalize their literacy knowledge (Cambourne, 1988; Harste et al., 1984).

Planning interactive read-alouds

Most students love to hear stories read aloud and look forward to storytime. They readily engage with good books read aloud by a teacher who enjoys books and the read-aloud experience. The teacher can enhance the read-aloud experience by leading children to engage with aspects of reading that contribute to the meaning-making process. Through ongoing interaction during read-alouds teachers can target key literary and process information for the ultimate purpose of supporting richer individual response to stories. Surprisingly, however, the practice of using ongoing conversation to engage students with reading process information and to bring response into the social realm is more challenging than it may first appear. Eeds and Peterson (1991) found that teachers were unsure about conducting literary conversations with their students. Goldberg (1992/1993) states that conversations between students and teachers that aim to instruct are intellectually demanding and do not come easily or naturally. Teachers who want to implement interactive read-alouds may find the following suggestions helpful in planning and conducting them.

Selecting books

High-interest picture books with rich language, absorbing plots, lively characters, and *multiple layers of meaning* will simultaneously promote pleasure and opportunity for learning. Very simple or highly familiar books may not successfully sustain meaningful interaction. Likewise, highly complex stories are unlikely to generate interactions that promote a pleasurable reading experience. For optimal engagement, review your favorite children's books and choose those that you love and that are suited to your students' interests.

Preparing for successful interactive read-alouds

Choosing an appropriate book does not ensure successful interactive read-alouds. Natural and meaningful engagement with stories is a result of thorough behind-the-scenes preparation.

1. *Read the book several times to yourself.* Take the time that is necessary to thoroughly understand and appreciate the book. Many children's books that appear simplistic on the surface are often quite complex. Think about the characters in the story; the structure of the text; the plot conflicts and resolutions; and the language the author has used to create the characters, the story, and the images. Articulate possible themes. Notice the point of view and setting. Ask yourself why these were chosen and how they are at work in the story. Examine the illustrations. Recognize where they enrich and add the story. Notice where they clearly illustrate the events and characters in the text. It is time consuming but enjoyable to review the book from multiple dimensions. Use this time to kindle your own intrigue with the literary artistic nature of the book.

2. *Think about the reading goals you have for your students and identify the process and strategy information at work in the story.* Review some of the aims you have for your students as developing readers. What meaning-making strategies do you want the students to use? Do you want to emphasize utilizing text structure, identifying with a character's feelings and actions, summarizing the story, predicting, identifying and interpreting themes, critiquing and reflecting on the plot, or learning to ask questions when meaning breaks down? What goals are especially relevant to this particular text? When you pause to recall your instructional goals, you are compelled to think about storybook reading as a context for engaging students in reading demonstrations, students' current instructional needs, and what goals are appropriately taught in relation to the story you have selected.

3. *Identify where students predictions about the developing story should be sought and shared.* Having students make and share predictions at critical points in the story will create the opportunity for them to figure the story out for themselves. Anticipate, before you read to the class, moments when you can assist readers in constructing a "wise" interpretation of the story (Wolf, 1988). Predicting helps students recognize and think about how stories work—how they are put together—which helps them read like experts. Predicting activates students' background knowledge and experiences, which prepares them to compare their own feelings and experiences with those in the story. Comparing and contrasting feelings and experiences make the story relevant to students.

4. *Anticipate where you may need to build students' background knowledge.* Often stories will contain references to concepts or information with which some but not all of students will have had experience. Consider at what points in the reading the information should be addressed (before or during the story) and consider to what extent it should be discussed.

5. *Think through how you will phrase your questions and predicting invitation, and anticipate student responses.* Surprisingly, even after all of the above preparation, as you first begin to implement interactive read-alouds, you may not automatically articulate well phrased questions. Initially, you might try writing clearly phrased questions onto the pages of the book. Then think about how your students might respond to the questions and predicting invitations. Realize that students will range in their ability to offer perceptive insights. Also realize that what is easily and accurately predicted by an adult is not necessarily easily or accurately predicted by young students. Value your student responses and use them as windows for peering into their thinking.

6. *After you have planned the read-aloud event, be prepared to relinquish your plains.* Above all, interactive read-aloud events should be responsive to the students. Be prepared to tailor your questions and comments to the dialogue that develops. In one interactive read-aloud that I observed, the teacher and I were both overwhelmed at the level of student interaction. They identified ideas that neither of us had discovered in the story. To the credit of the teacher, she was very responsive to their ideas and helped students explore them throughout the reading of the book, even though she spent extra minutes on storytime that day.

7. *After reading, devise opportunities for students to explore stories in personal and exciting ways.* Very often it is appropriate to follow interactive readings with discussion that further explores student response to the story. These discussions allow for greater personalization of stories, whereas interactive readings tend to focus on building a shared meaning. In addition to after-reading discussion, follow-up activities can lead to meaningful exploration. For instance, after the *Blueberries for Sal* reading. Mrs. Herbert arranged for the classroom paraprofessional to assist groups of 5–6 students in making blueberry pancakes. This extended the students' connection to Sal's feelings—now they could relate to the delight of eating the berries! Writing, art, music, and drama also lead to literacy growth and meaningful exploration.

Other considerations

Classrooms are complex environments, and it is often the inconspicuous details that support successful lessons. Two inconspicuous but important details are at work in successful interactive read-alouds: time and good judgment.

Set aside an adequate amount of class time to conduct interactive read-alouds. Reading a story interactively will approximately double the amount of time it would take to read the story in a straight-through format. If you plan adequate time for reading, you will resist the tendency to rush the event and limit student interaction. And use good judgment about the amount of interaction to include during reading. Excessive dialogue may disrupt the enjoyment of a story. Funding the appropriate amount of dialogue will evolve with your experience and with students' realization that storytime is also talk time.

Conclusion

Clearly, many elements contribute to successful interactive readings, but there is no formula for success. In each event, idiosyncrasies of the students, the story, and the teacher lead to engaging with reading in fresh ways. Dialogue during read-aloud events supports students as they construct meaning based on the story and their personal experiences. These meaning-centered interactions engage students with literary information and demonstrate strategies that they can adopt for use when reading independently. Not every read-aloud event need be interactive, but this approach to reading aloud provides a way to expand teachers' techniques for engaging students with books and literary information.

References

Barrentine, S. J. (1993). *Teacher's comprehension building practices during storybook reading events.* Unpublished doctoral dissertation, University of California, Los Angeles.

Cambourne, B. (1988). *The whole story: Natural learning and the acquisition of literacy in the classroom.* Auckland, New Zealand: Ashton Scholastic.

Dole, J. A., Duffy, G. G., Roehler, L. R., & Pearson, P. D. (1991). Moving from the old to the new: Research on reading comprehension instruction. *Review of Educational Research, 61,* 239–264.

Eeds, M., & Peterson, R. (1991). Teacher as curator: Learning to talk about literature. *The Reading Teachers, 45,* 118–126.

Goldenberg, C. (1992/1993). Instructional conversations: Promoting comprehension through discussion. *The Reading Teacher, 46,* 316–326.

Harker, J. O. (1988). Contrasting the content of two storyreading lessons: A propositional analysis. In J. L. Green & J. O. Harker (Eds.). *Multiple perspective analyses of classroom discourse* (pp. 49–70). Norwood, NJ: Ablex.

Harste, J. C., Woodward, V. A., & Burke, C. L. (1984). *Language stories and literacy lessons.* Portsmouth, NH: Heinemann.

Holdaway, D. (1979). *The foundations of literacy.* Sydney, Australia: Ashton Scholastic.

Martinez, M. G., and Teale, W. H. (1993). Teacher storybook reading style: A comparison of six teachers. *Research in the Teaching of English, 27,* 175–199.

Mason, J. M., Peterman, C. L., & Kerr, B. M. (1988). Reading to kindergarten children. In D. S. Strickland & L. M. Morrow (Eds.). *Emerging literacy: Young children learn to read and write* (pp. 52–62). Newark, DE: International Reading Association.

Mathie, V. (1995). Making beliefs explicit: One teacher's journey. In B. Cambourne & J. Turbill (Eds.), *Responsive evaluation: Making valid judgments about student literacy* (pp. 28–37). Portsmouth, NH: Heinemann.

McCloskey, R. (1948). *Blueberries for Sal.* New York: Viking.

McGee, L. M. (1995). Talking about books. In N. L. Roser & M. G. Martinez (Eds.). *Book talk and beyond: Children and teachers respond to literature* (pp. 105–115). Newark, DE: International Reading Association.

Moss, J. F. (1995). Preparing focus units with literature: Crafty foxes and authors' craft. In N. L. Roser & M. G. Martinez (Eds.), *Book talk and beyond: Children and teachers respond to literature* (pp. 63–65). Newark, DE: International Reading Association.

Peterson, R., & Eeds, M. (1990). *Grand conversations: Literature groups in action.* New York: Scholastic.

Smith, K. (1990). Entertaining a text. In K. G. Short & K. M. Pierce (Eds.). *Talking about books: Creating literate communities* (pp. 17–31). Portsmouth, NH: Heinemann.

Whitin, D. J., & Wilde, S. (1992). *Read any good math lately? Children's books for mathematical learning, K–6.* Portsmouth, NH: Heinemann.

Wolf, D. P. (1986). *Reading reconsidered: Literature and literacy in high school.* New York: College Board Publications.

C.A.S.H.
Exit Slip

Cognitive/**I**ntellectual—List one thing you learned from today's session.

Affective—How do you feel about what you learned today?

Surprised—What surprised you?

Helpful—What did you find helpful?

Chapter 9

Questioning

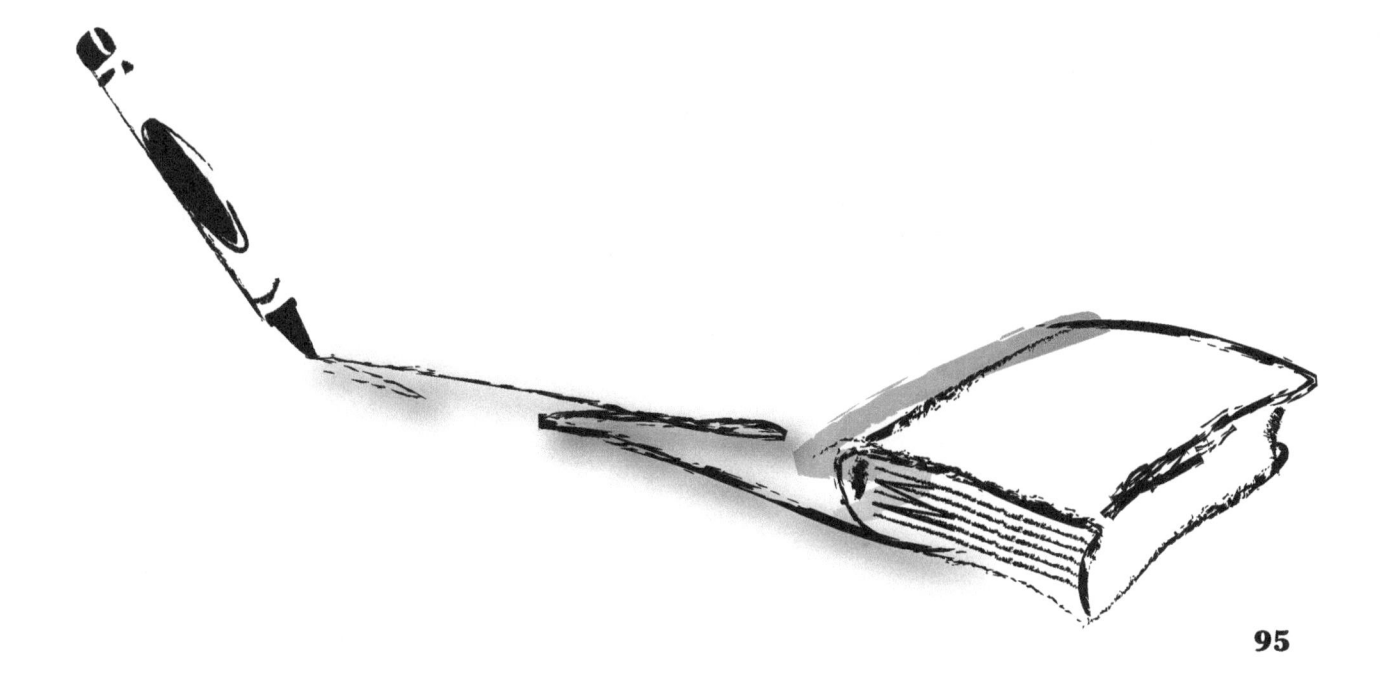

Why Ask Questions?

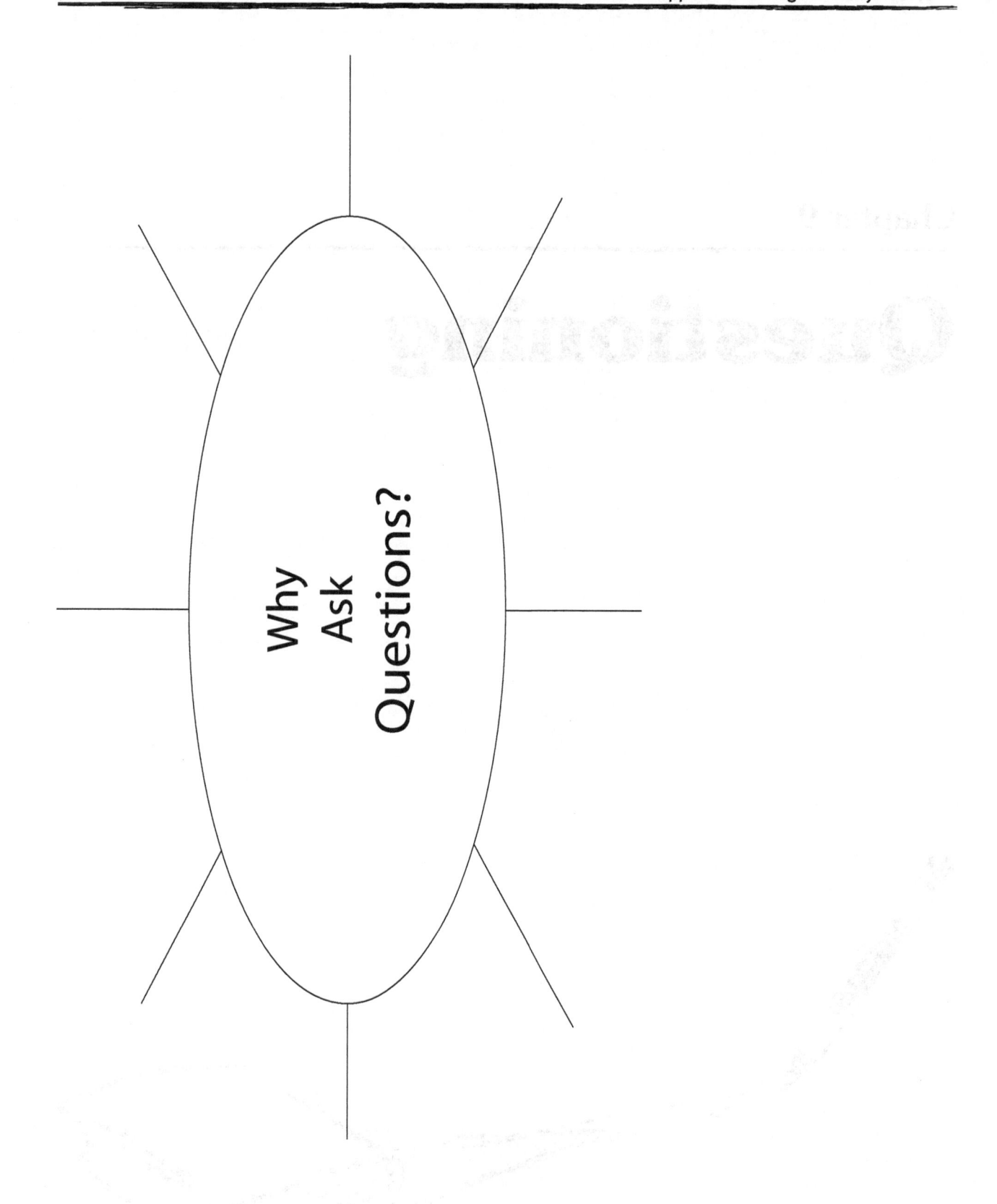

King Penguin Babies

Did you know that King Penguins have only one baby every two years? In the middle of November, the female King Penguin lays her egg, and then the male and female take turns taking good care of it. In January, the chick is ready to come out and begins to peck through its shell. It takes two days until the naked grey chick finally breaks out of the shell. It grows a thick, warm, brown coat of fur after three weeks. You might say it looks very much like a teddy bear with a beak! By October, the chick begins to molt. It loses its "fur coat" as it grows new feathers underneath. Until the King Penguin is two years old, it has a black beak and yellow markings. When it is full grown, it has the orange markings which are unique to its kind.

Literal question:

Inferential question:

Applied question:

"Penguins" Image © 2008 by Stawek. Used under license from Shutterstock, inc.

K-W-L

TOPIC:

What I Know	What I Want to Know	What I Learned

Ogle, D. M. (1986). KWL-A teaching model that develops active reading of expository text. *The Reading Teacher*, vol 39, 564–571.

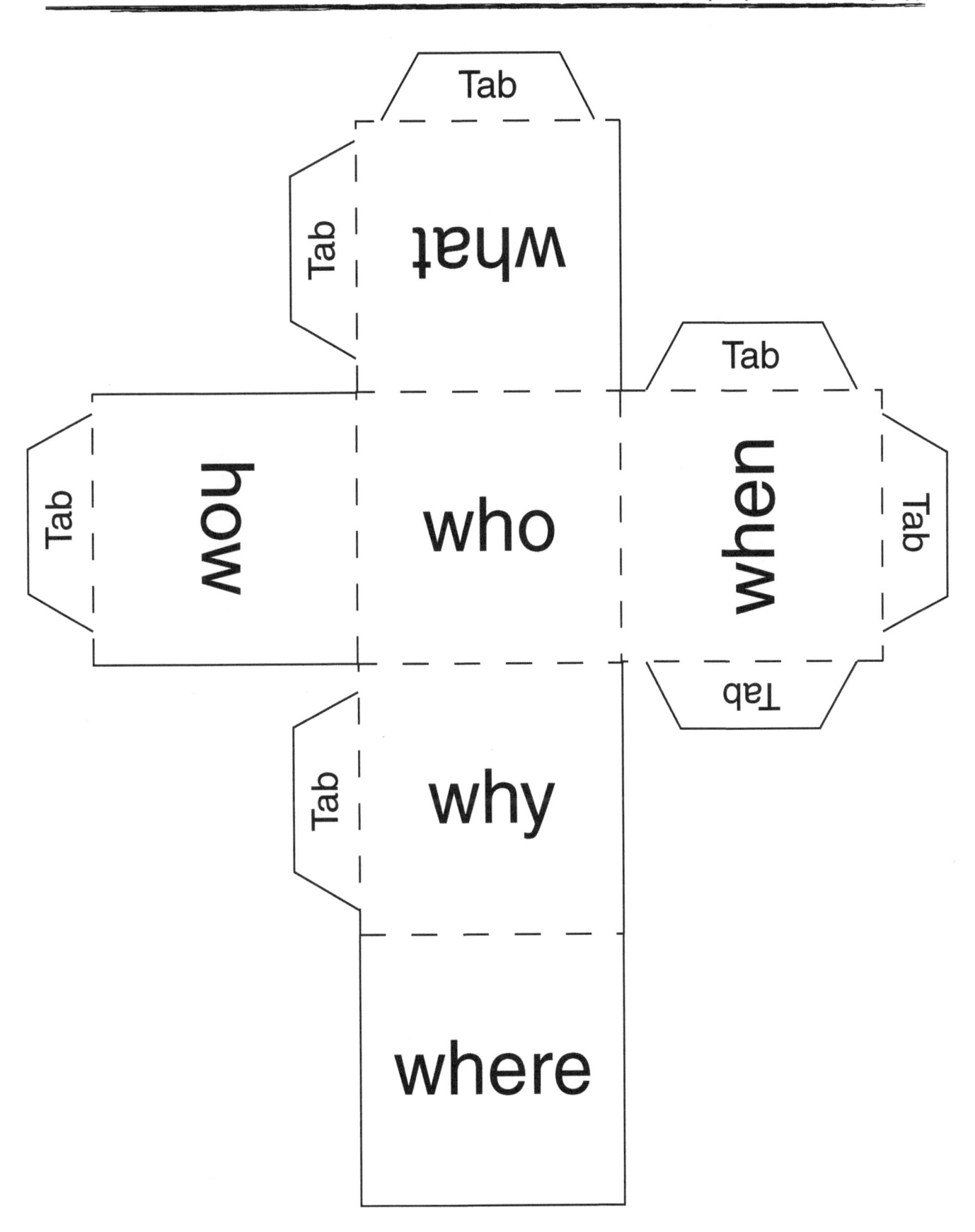

Chapter 9 Questioning 99

what | who | when | why | where | how | Tab

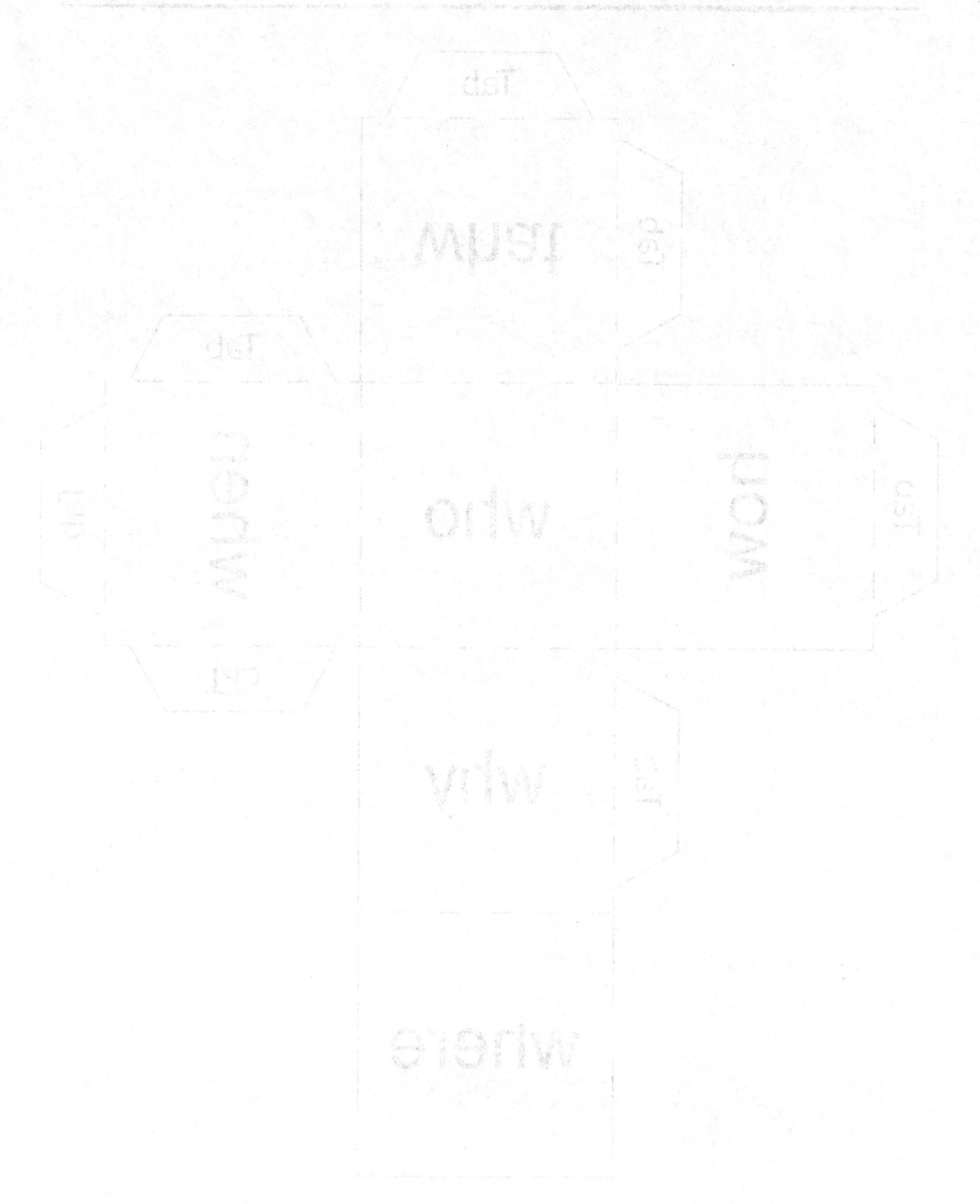

Chapter 2 Questioning

Cube template (unfolded)

- what
- who
- how
- why
- where
- what (top)

(Tabs on edges)

Chapter 10

Reading in the Content Areas

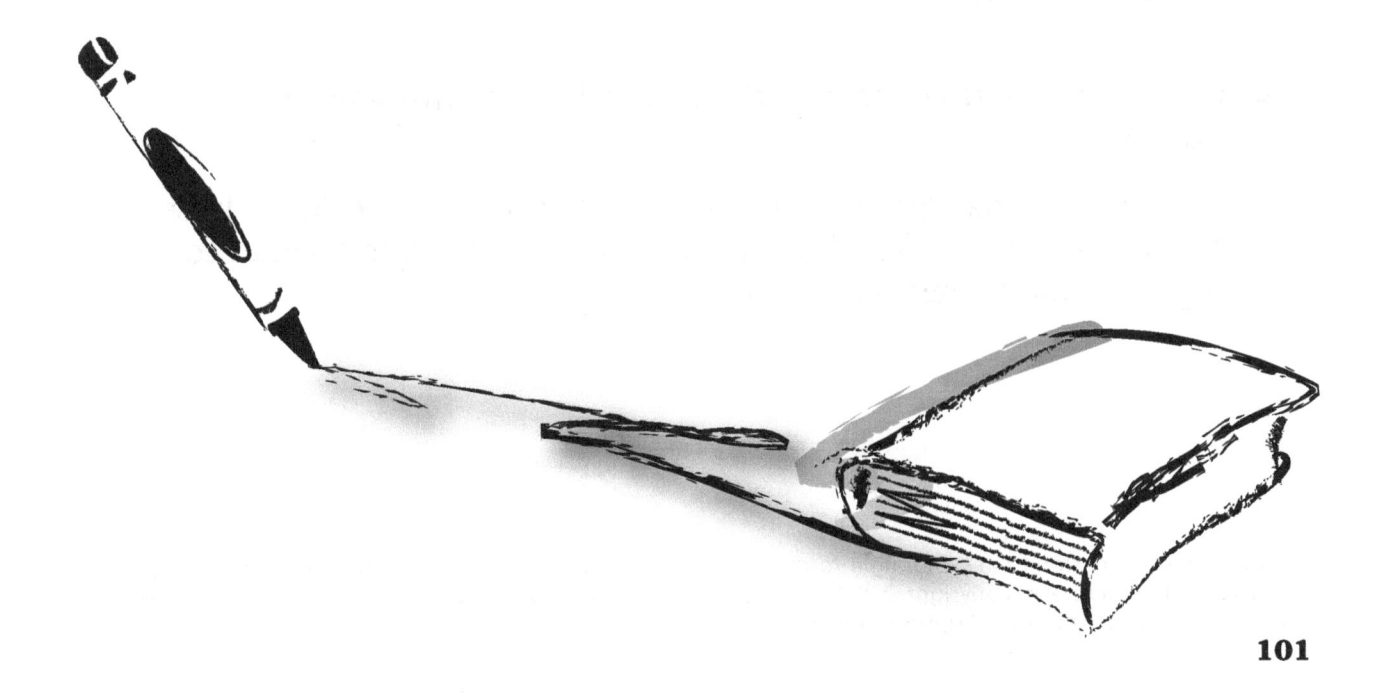

Six Serious Reasons to Include Informational Text in the Classroom

1. Informational text is key to success in later schooling.

    Including more informational text in early schooling may put children in a better position to handle the reading and writing demands of later schooling. Children should "read to learn" and "learn to read" from the earliest grades and throughout their school careers.

2. Informational text is ubiquitous in the larger society.

    As adults, we read a great deal of nonfiction in our workplaces, homes, and communities. At least 96% of the text on the World Wide Web is expository. If we are going to prepare children for this world, we need to be very serious about teaching them to read and write informational text.

3. Informational text is preferred reading for some children.

    Including more informational text in classrooms may improve attitudes toward reading and even serve as a catalyst for overall literacy development.

4. Informational text often addresses children's interests and questions.

    Approaches that emphasize reading for the purpose of addressing real questions children have about their world tend to lead to higher achievement and motivation.

Reprinted with permission from *Exploring Informational Texts: From Theory to Practice* by Linda Hoyt, Margaret Mooney and Brenda Parkes. Copyright © 2003 by Linda Hoyt, Margaret Mooney, Brenda Parkes. Published by Heinemann, Portsmouth, NH. All rights reserved.

5. Informational text builds knowledge of the natural and social world.

   Reading and listening to informational text can develop children's knowledge of the world around them. This in turn can promote children's comprehension of subsequent texts they read, as higher background knowledge is associated with higher comprehension.

6. Informational text has many important text features.

   Informational text may be particularly well-suited to building vocabulary. Informational text also includes a number of graphical devices: learning to read those may support children's overall visual literacy development.

104 Read! Write! Discuss! Learn! A Workbook of Interactive Handouts to Support the College Literacy Course

Journey Through Your Textbook

Your textbook is a valuable source of information, if you know what it contains and how to use it! Get to know your _____ by jumping from stone to stone through the river below with a partner. Use the back of this sheet for each answer, then color each stepping stone as you complete each task.

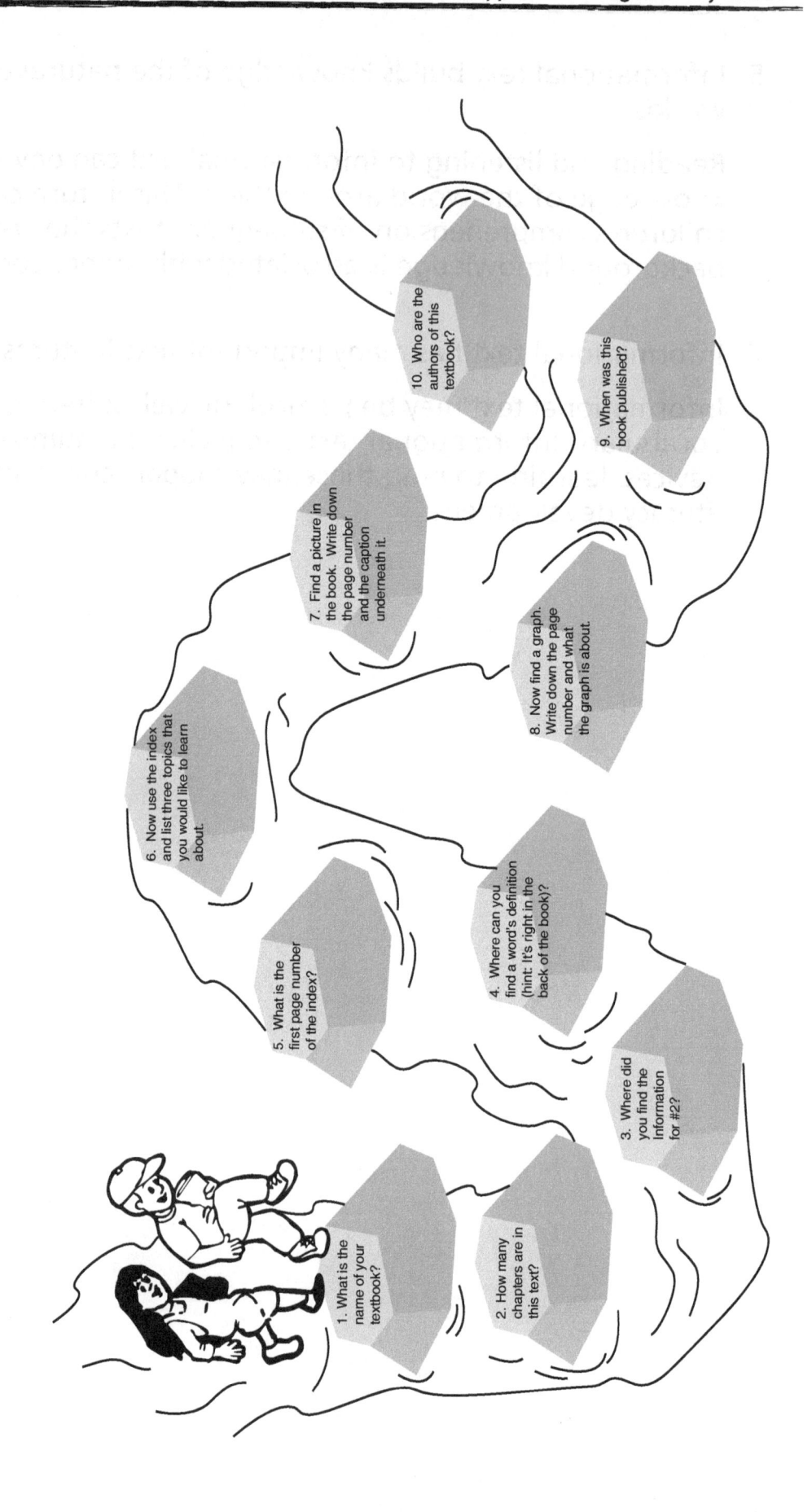

1. What is the name of your textbook?

2. How many chapters are in this text?

3. Where did you find the information for #2?

4. Where can you find a word's definition (hint: It's right in the back of the book)?

5. What is the first page number of the index?

6. Now use the index and list three topics that you would like to learn about.

7. Find a picture in the book. Write down the page number and the caption underneath it.

8. Now find a graph. Write down the page number and what the graph is about.

9. When was this book published?

10. Who are the authors of this textbook?

Technical Vocabulary Terms Across the Curriculum

Math	Science	Geography	Health	Social Studies	English	Music

Anticipation Guide

Before			After	
T	F		T	F
		1. The Great Wall of China took 500 years to build.		
		2. The wall is made of stone, brick, marble, and earth.		
		3. The wall was built to provide a scenic view for its residents.		
		4. After the wall was in ruins, it was restored in the early 1900's.		
		5. It is considered one of the greatest constructions ever built.		

(sing to the tune of Head, Shoulders, Knees, and Toes)

Egg, tadpole, froglet, frog, froglet, frog!
Egg, tadpole, froglet, frog, froglet, frog . . .
Metamorphosis is the change that they go through!
Egg, tadpole, froglet, frog, froglet, frog!

Write a song for "King Penguin Babies" on page 97.

Chapter 11

The Reading-Writing Connection

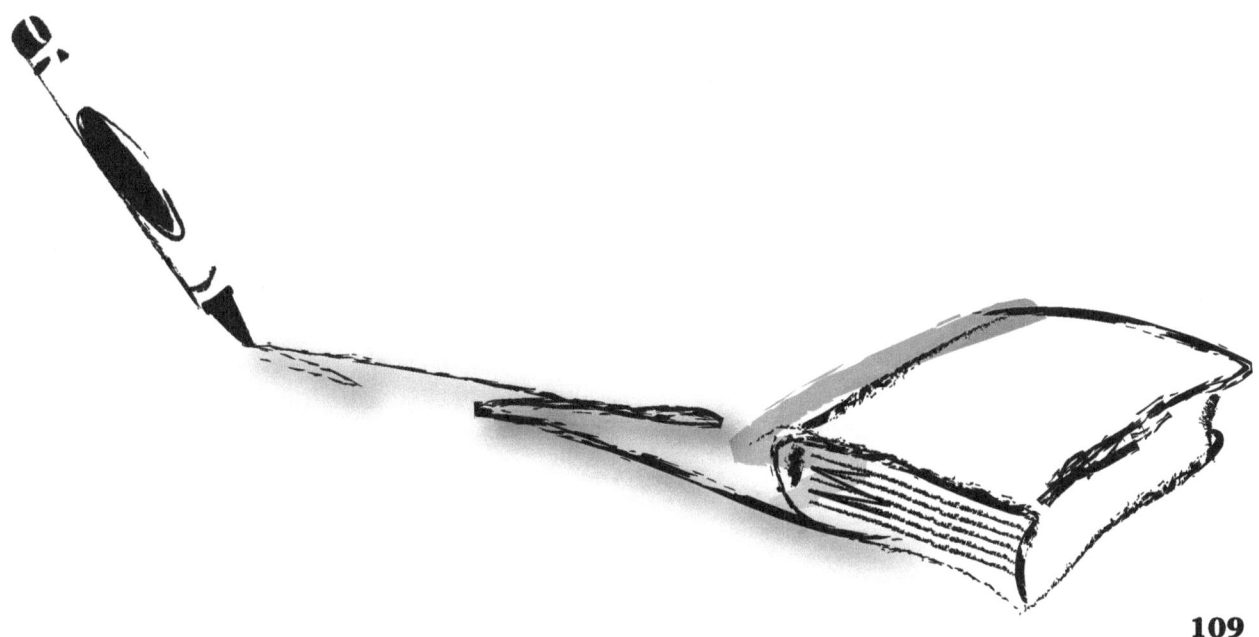

What Could You Write about Today?

- Bullying
- marriage
- love
- LGBTQ relationships
- Suicide prevention
- pets
- depression
-
-
-
-

Choose One Topic and Web It Below

- prom
- Selfharm
- medication
- Bullying
- LGBTQ
- Sorority

Chapter 11   The Reading-Writing Connection

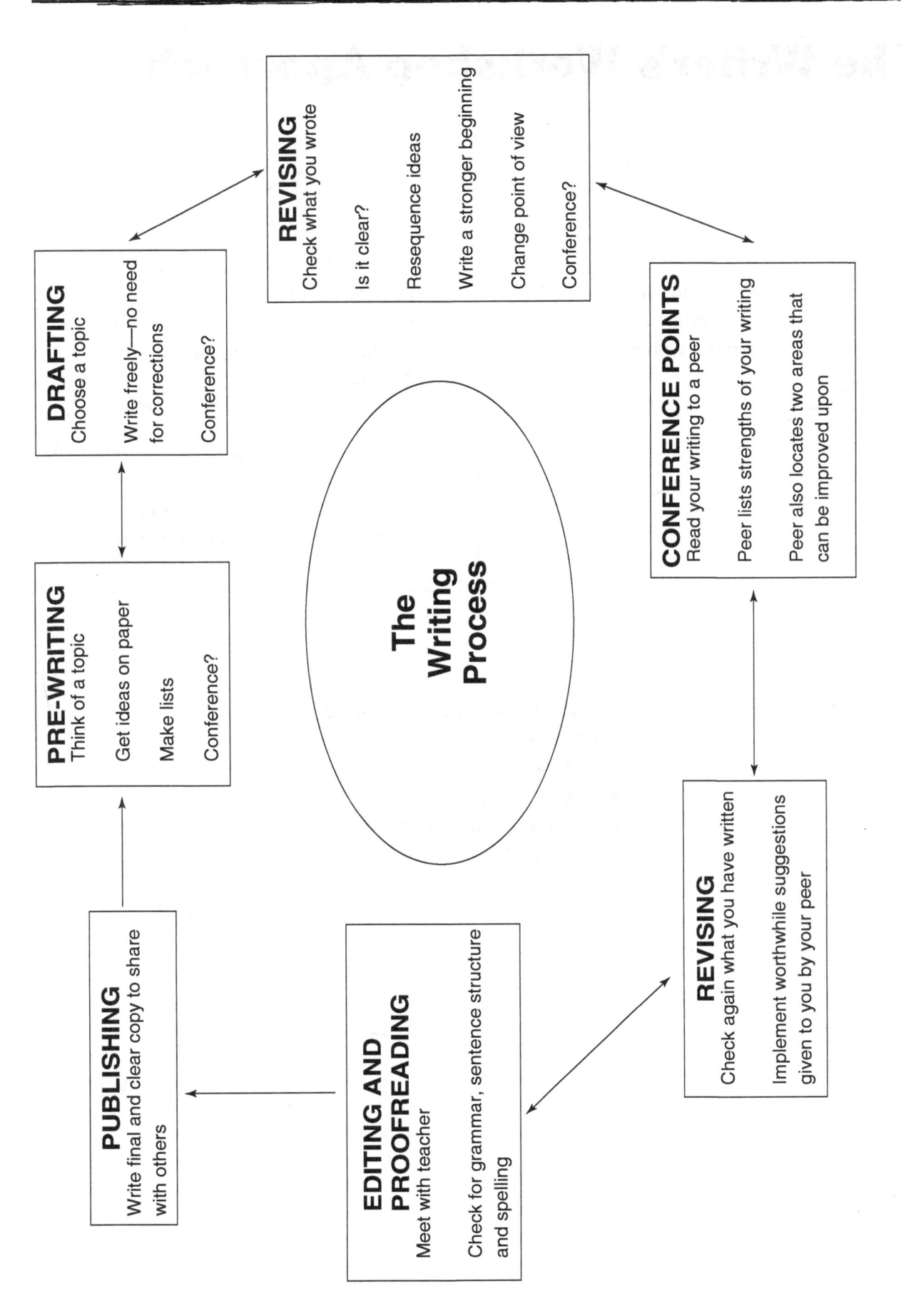

The Writing Process

PRE-WRITING
Think of a topic
Get ideas on paper
Make lists
Conference?

DRAFTING
Choose a topic
Write freely—no need for corrections
Conference?

REVISING
Check what you wrote
Is it clear?
Resequence ideas
Write a stronger beginning
Change point of view
Conference?

CONFERENCE POINTS
Read your writing to a peer
Peer lists strengths of your writing
Peer also locates two areas that can be improved upon

REVISING
Check again what you have written
Implement worthwhile suggestions given to you by your peer

EDITING AND PROOFREADING
Meet with teacher
Check for grammar, sentence structure and spelling

PUBLISHING
Write final and clear copy to share with others

Graves, Donald (1983). *Writing: Teachers and Children at Work*. Portsmouth, NH: Heineman

The Writer's Workshop Approach

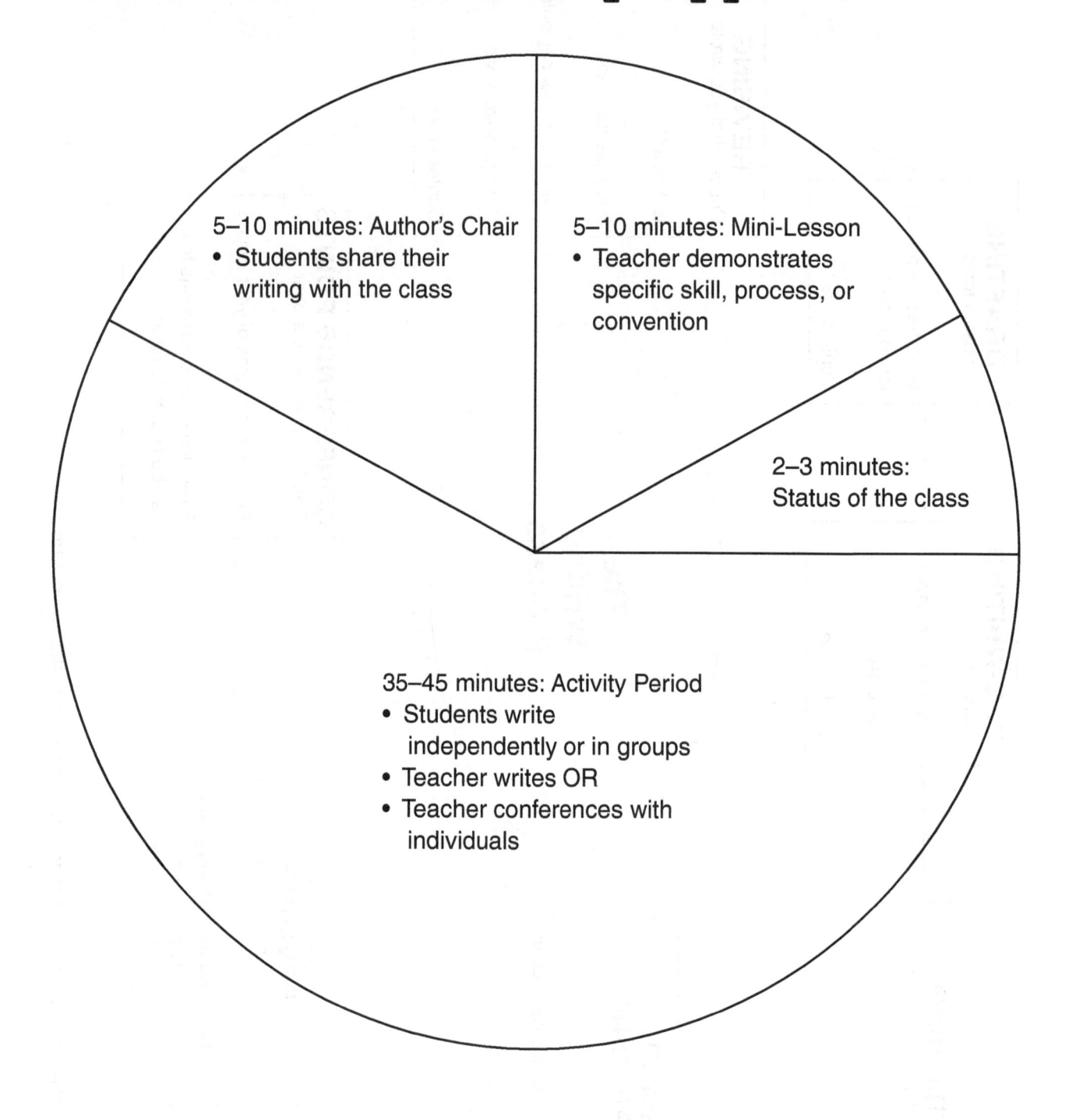

5–10 minutes: Author's Chair
- Students share their writing with the class

5–10 minutes: Mini-Lesson
- Teacher demonstrates specific skill, process, or convention

2–3 minutes: Status of the class

35–45 minutes: Activity Period
- Students write independently or in groups
- Teacher writes OR
- Teacher conferences with individuals

Purposes and Ideas for Writing

Purpose for Writing	General Description of Possible Writing Activities
to entertain	<ul><li>create a new ending or beginning for the story</li><li>retell the story in your own words</li><li>create a parody of the prompt</li><li>create a rhyme, poem, or patter based on the reading</li></ul>
to persuade	<ul><li>write a letter to one of the story's characters, giving advice or requesting help</li><li>write a critical essay about the prompt</li><li>write an editorial based on the prompt</li></ul>
to learn	<ul><li>retell an important event, process, or situation</li><li>summarize or synthesize texts</li><li>report on a phenomenon mentioned in the text</li></ul>
to inform	<ul><li>report on a phenomenon mentioned in the text</li><li>construct directions or instructions based on something that happens in the text</li><li>describe and prepare a critique of the text</li></ul>
to evoke feelings	<ul><li>describe a personal experience that relates to the text</li><li>give an account of what a character might think or feel</li><li>create a journal or diary entry for a character</li><li>write a letter to a story character or the author of the prompt</li></ul>

Writing Domains

Focus

- Think of a camera focusing on one thing.
- Write about one topic only.

Content

- This is the main idea and its details.
- This is the parts of the picture.

Organization

- The story has a beginning, middle, and end.
- The story is in the correct order.
- This is like the pictures in an album being in the order that they happened.

Style

- This is color versus black and white in a picture.
- You want to add more color to your story.
- Show what your characters do, don't just tell what they do.

Conventions

- These are the touch-ups to your story.
- Conventions include spelling, punctuation, capitalization, indenting for paragraphs and quotations, quotation marks, and complete sentences.

Adapted with permission from Barbara Heister and Sue Mowery.

Writing Prompts

These questions are designed to facilitate students' imaginations and sharpen their critical thinking skills.

If you could change one thing about your life to make it better, what would it be?

If you could be any TV character at all, who would you be? Why?

If you had the power to turn yourself into an animal anytime you wish, which animal would you choose to turn into and why?

If you could suddenly give yourself a talent that you don't presently have, what would it be?

What is the most interesting gift you've ever received?

If you saw a kitten by the roadside, what would you do? If you knew your parents wouldn't allow you to keep the kitten, what other actions might you take to help it?

Do you think our environment would be in such danger today if more people had started thinking about conservation and recycling 50 years ago?

Did you ever get blamed for something you didn't do? How did it make you feel?

If you were the principal of your school, what's the first new rule you would make?

Group: _____

| Main | Points |
| Support | Support |

topic

Five-Step Editing

Types of Journals

1. Dialogue journals

2. Buddy journals

3. Double entry journals

4. Response journals

5. Key-pal correspondence journals

Dialogue Journal Writing

Directions:

1. Two peers will write and discuss the topic of field experience.

2. You will write about your concerns, excitement, and questions.

3. As you write you will acknowledge one another's ideas and continue to elaborate for at least 2 journal entries.

Why do we assess children?

- to keep content cumulative
- to check knowledge
- to keep schools accountable
- to allocate funds
- to create a uniform education
- to determine possible needed services
- teacher analysis
- to evaluate the curriculum

Chapter 12

Literacy Assessment

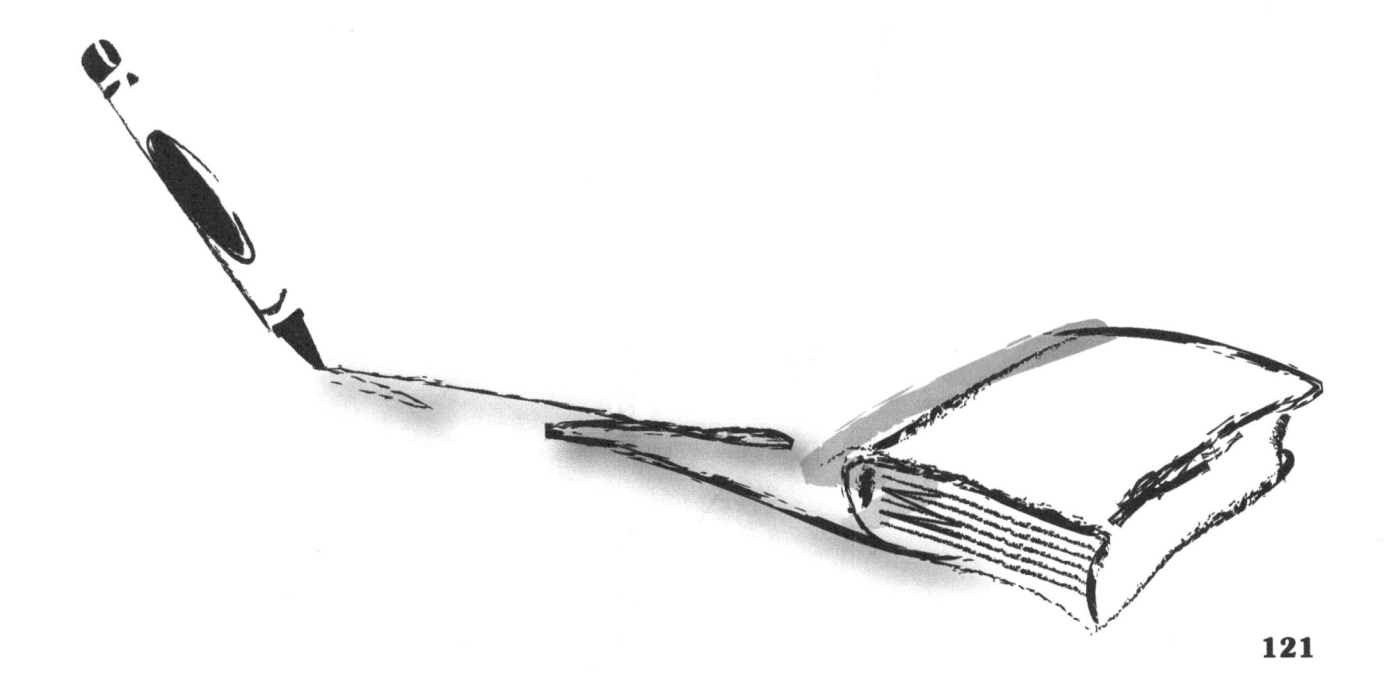

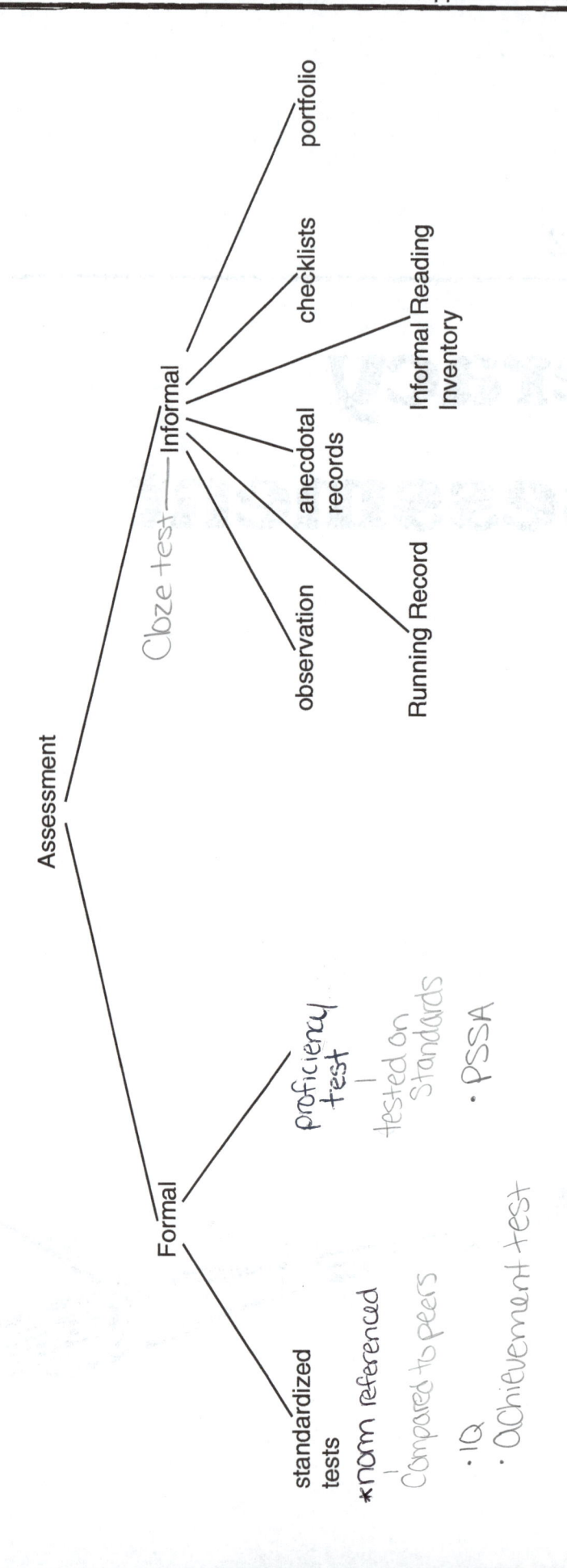

Assessment

Formal
- standardized tests
  - *norm referenced
  - Compared to peers
    - IQ
    - achievement test
- proficiency test
  - tested on standards
    - PSSA

Informal
— Cloze test
- observation
- anecdotal records
- checklists
- Running Record
- Informal Reading Inventory
- portfolio

Assessment Activity

Directions

1. Review the passage seen below.
2. Connect this passage to points made in the class lecture.
3. Determine the most appropriate response for each blank.
4. Use each term only once.

The trends for evaluating literacy today involve both 1. _____ and 2. _____ assessment. Ever since, "No Child Left Behind," the focus has been placed on more formal type testing. However it is still essential for a teacher to recognize various types of informal assessments. Informal record keeping includes such procedures as 3. _____ and 4. _____. An error that considers the extent to which a child uses graphic-sound, syntactic, and semantic information is known as a 5. _____. The informal evaluation that was developed by Marie Clay to assess fluency and which is given to beginning readers is the 6. _____. Another informal assessment that assures active student thinking about their own assessment process is the use of the 7. _____. Finally an assessment that is most thorough (as it includes questions along with varied types of oral reading errors) and that has three criteria levels is known as the 8. _____.

   The most formal type of assessment is the 9. _____ test, which is used to 10. _____ one student's ability to that of another student. Another type of formal assessment is the 11. _____, which focuses on the mastery of reading skills, as they are related to specific objectives. A more realistic assessment trend is to attempt to evaluate the child in a more authentic way. This is done so as to encourage students to read more 12. _____, rather than to have them focus only on isolated skills.

Word Bank: portfolio; anecdotal records; running record; standardized testing; informal reading inventory; strategically; metacognitive process; to compare; High Stakes Testing; miscue analysis; kidwatching notes; criterion-referenced test

Running Records

The use of running records for text reading was developed by New Zealand educator Marie Clay. The main purpose for this informal assessment was to provide a way for a teacher to observe, record, and analyze what a child does during the process of reading. The teacher assumes the role of an observer, so as to be able to form a record of the child's independent reading behavior.

Procedures:

1. The child reads orally from both a familiar and unfamiliar text.

2. The reading process usually proceeds as a child reads independently, however, the teacher is permitted to supply a word if the child has a lengthy pause.

3. While the child is reading, the teacher observes and makes a note of various reading behaviors such as: repetitions, self-corrections, substitutions, insertions and omissions. Also, behaviors such as long pauses or asking for help should be recognized. The teacher will record these errors by using a system similar to the one used in the Informal Reading Inventory.

4. After reading, the teacher then analyzes what she or he has recorded and makes inferences as to what type of cues the child missed. The teacher will also note whether or not the child made use of any type of reading strategies. (miscue analysis—self corrections)

5. This type of analysis enables the teacher to make instructional decisions about how to assist a child during future reading experiences. Usually a passage to be used for the running record will consist of between 100 and 200 words.

Reasons for Doing a Running Record

1. Provides an accurate and objective description of what actually occurs in the course of reading

2. Provides diagnostic information on how the reader is processing print

3. Indicates what a reader knows/can do

4. Provides insights about what needs to be learned next

5. Provides qualitative as well as quantitative information

6. Provides a picture of progress over time

7. Allows the teacher to make informed decisions concerning:
   - instructional needs
   - grouping
   - reading levels
   - suitable materials

8. Allows the teacher to monitor effectiveness of program emphasis/mini lessons

9. Provides documented information for other teachers, administrators, parents, etc.

Conventions

- Accurate reading ✓ ✓ ✓

- Substitution $\dfrac{\text{went}}{\text{want}}$ $\left(\dfrac{\text{child}}{\text{text}}\right)$

- Repetition (R) R or $\dfrac{}{\text{✓ ✓ R}}$

- Self-correction (SC) $\dfrac{\text{went}}{\text{want}}\bigg|\text{SC}$

- Omission $\dfrac{-}{\text{very}}$

- Insertion $\dfrac{\text{little}}{-}$

- Told (T) $\dfrac{}{\text{thought}}\bigg|\text{T}$

- Appeal (A) $\dfrac{}{\text{sometimes}}\bigg|\text{A}$

- TTA Try that again [TTA]

Reprinted with permission from *An Observation Survey of Early Literacy Achievement* by Marie M. Clay. Copyright © 2003 by Marie M. Clay. Published by Heinemann, Portsmouth, NH. All rights reserved.

Directions

Code the following passage.
Use the Running Record scoring system as you decode.

"Peter, why aren't you smiling?" asked Dad.

"This will be a fun day for all of us."

"Your sister has a birthday."

"I am not happy", said Peter

"I want to get a special gift for my sister."

"What kind of gift is special to you?" Dad asked.

"Your sister will like whatever gift you give her."

"Do you think I can make something for her?" asked Peter

"What a wonderful idea," said Dad.

"I will go in the house right now." said Peter.

"I will think of a nice gift for my sister."

Number of Words—95

Running Record

Independent level (easy to read) text   95% to 100% correct

Instructional level text   90% to 94% correct

Frustration level (difficult) text   Less than 89% correct

Exit Slip

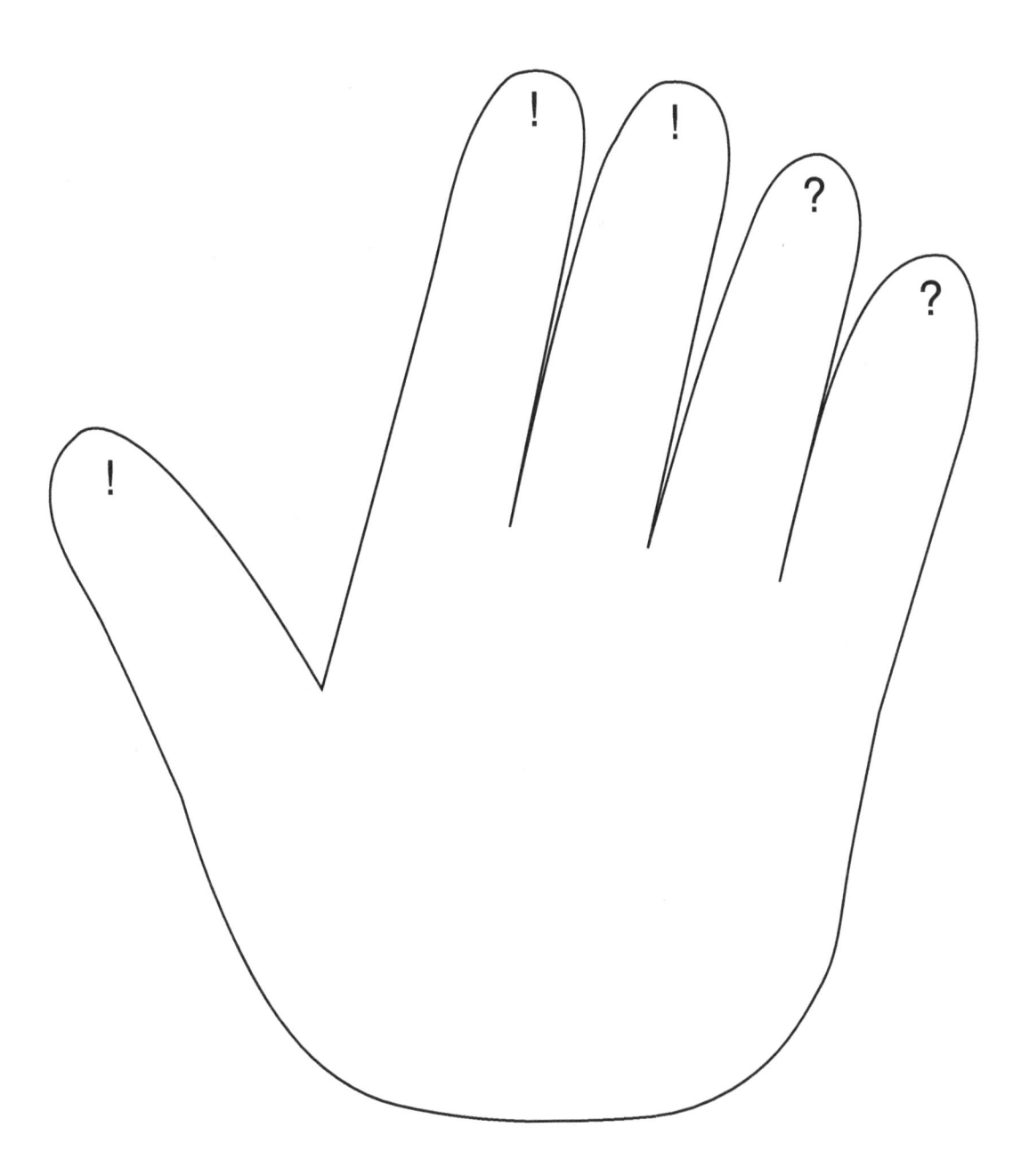

Chapter 13

Diverse Learners

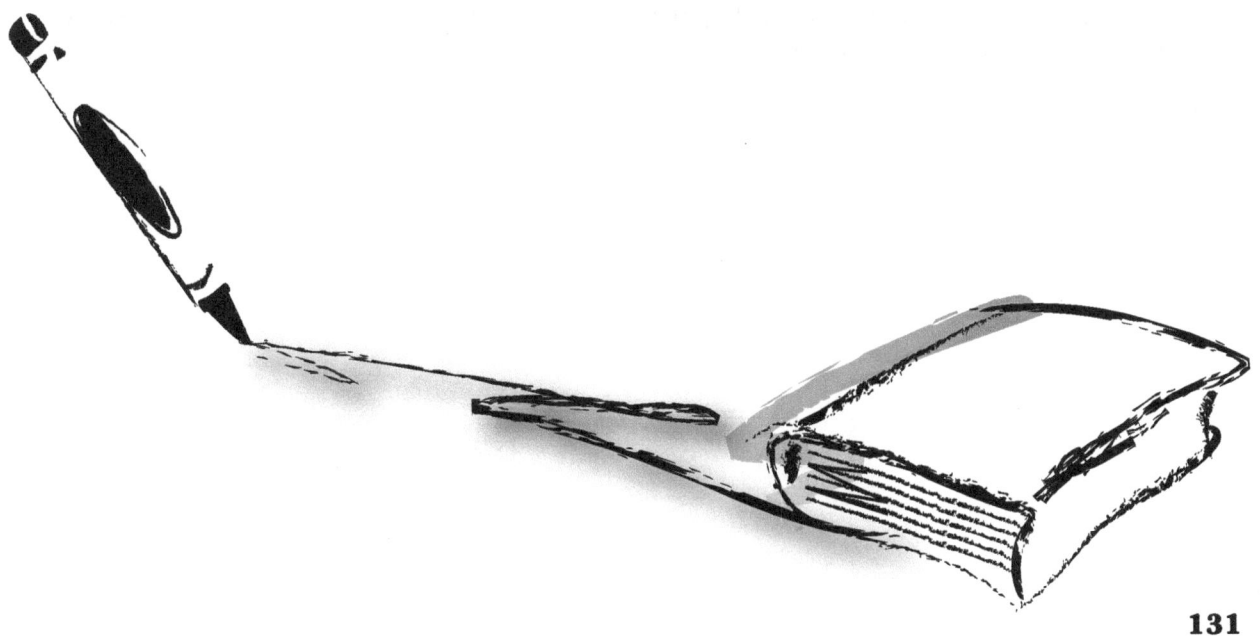

Accommodations/Modifications Quiz

1. Social Studies test is read aloud to student. (Accommodation) Modification

2. Student is required to master double-digit addition and subtraction without regrouping while the rest of the class is required to master double-digit addition and subtraction with regrouping. Accommodation (Modification)

3. A peer tutor is provided for a student. (Accommodation) Modification

4. Student is allowed to use manipulatives to solve science problems. (Accommodation) Modification

5. Student is required to read and write decimals while the rest of the class is required to also compare, order, add, and subtract decimals. Accommodation (Modification)

6. Student is given grid paper to rewrite science experiment. (Accommodation) Modification

7. Student is given 10 instead of 20 problems for homework. Accommodation (Modification)

8. Social Studies test is given in sections. Student completes each section at a time and then reports to the teacher for the next section and the directions. (Accommodation) Modification

9. A first grader is expected only to count and identify numbers 1 to 20. Curriculum requires first graders to go up to 100. Accommodation (Modification)

10. Fourth-grade curriculum requires fourth graders to do long division into the thousands place. A fourth grader in your classroom is only required to act out basic division facts. Accommodation (Modification)

Adaptations

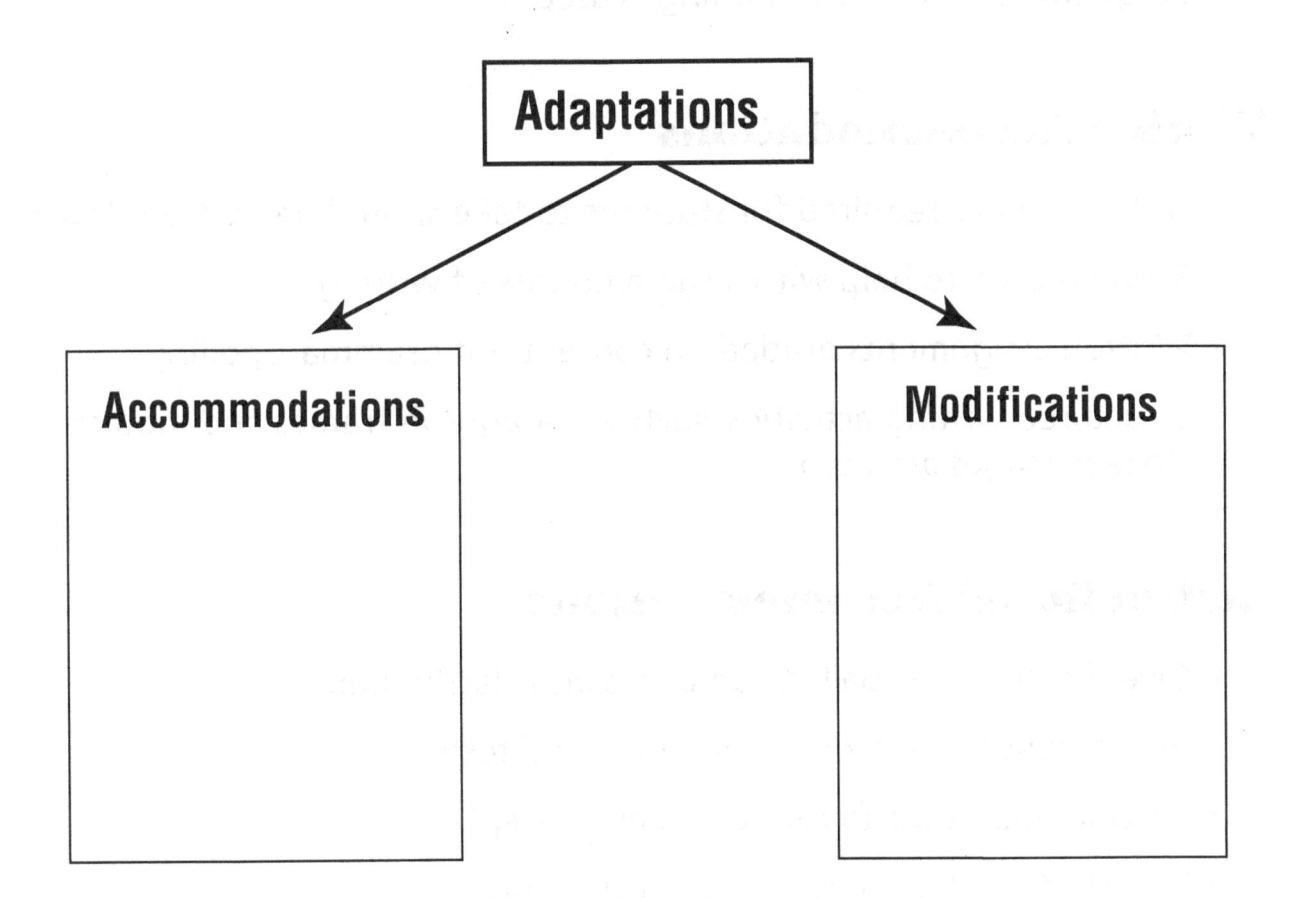

```
        Adaptations
        /        \
Accommodations   Modifications
```

So what is the difference between accommodations and modifications? Accommodations occur when a student has the SAME objectives as the rest of the class, but scaffolds are put in place in order to help the student be successful. Modifications occur when the child has FEWER objectives than the rest of the class, and/or the objectives are significantly altered.

Reading Accommodations

- Written material is read orally to student(s)
- In partner reading, low readers are paired with average readers
- Difficult reading given previously to student(s) for practice

- Reading material given to student(s) on tape
- Frequent variety of questioning is used

Writing Accommodations

- Notes that are required for students to take should be written down
- Scribe is used to help with large amounts of writing
- Written assignments graded on content not grammar/spelling
- Structured writing activities, such as paragraph frames and modified cloze passages are used

Instructional Accommodations

- Give directions verbally to students and clarify them
- Give extended time on assignments and tests
- Provide peer tutor to reinforce key concepts
- Seat student close to source of instruction
- When possible include the use of manipulatives
- Use study guides and outlines
- Reteach instruction when necessary

ABC Brainstorming

Topic: _____

A	B	C	D	E	F
G	H	I	J	K	L
M	N	O	P	Q	R
S	T	U	V	W	XYZ

Situations and Solutions for Students with Special Needs

1. Luis is a high functioning mildly mentally retarded [MR] student who is included in his third-grade classroom periodically during the day. He returns each day to his regular education homeroom after lunch. At that time his teacher is having reading workshop. Every student is to read silently and then write a response in his or her reading log. Each day the teacher then asks a select few to share their responses. Luis can read but he cannot read the chapter books his classmates are reading. He almost always rereads the same book for reading workshop. Luis can write but always seems to write the same message, "I like my book." He needs prompting to share verbally.

    Comments:
    - Teacher prompting
    - Similar topic books
    - Question cube

2. Mark has a learning disability [LD]. When he reads aloud, his reading accuracy seems equal to his fourth-grade classmates. However, he has significant difficulty with reading comprehension. He receives services in the learning support room to help him improve his understanding when reading. His fourth-grade homeroom teacher is using small guided reading groups with dynamic grouping as part of her reading program.

    Comments:
    - Communicate w/ learning support teacher
    - *his reading so he can pause + ponder by chunking

Chapter 13 Diverse Learners 137

3. Jerry's I.E.P. indicates that he is above level in reading and should be included for fifth-grade reading instruction. His family does not have a TV, but Jerry does not mind. He reads constantly. However, Jerry does not like to write. His teacher wants him to respond to all text in writing. She says that he will sit with a blank piece of paper in front of him for hours and refuses to write, stating, "I only like to read." Jerry's label is gifted LD. What can his teacher do to help this talented student reach his full potential in the language arts?

   Comments:
   - Verbally retells story
   - Computer
   - Scribe

4. Although Thomas enjoys a variety of genres, he cannot read on level. He has an excellent knowledge base and can remember facts and details from informational books. His fifth-grade teacher is reading a narrative book, *Where The Red Fern Grows,* for read-aloud. She has noted that when she is done reading and the children are engaged in conversation about the story, Thomas is able to join in and able to answer some inferential questions. What can be done?

   Comments:
   - provide pictures

5. Karla can't read; that is, she is a sixth-grade student who can only decode and spell words on a first-grade level. Karla has a good knowledge base and a 5–7 grade listening level depending upon the material. Her parents would like her to be included for all science and social studies lessons. Her teacher is wondering how a first-grade reader can read, work, and learn in a sixth-grade room. What can the teacher do to help her feel more included, increase her participation, and improve her reading and spelling skills?

   Comments:

6. Every year Miss Kelly is frustrated. She finds the same results each year when she tests the children in her primary classroom. It seems that somehow every year, the principal gives her 4–5 very low readers. She remembers that by the end of the year they all have improved, but never are able to catch up to the rest of the class and are still below grade level. Miss Kelly thinks that it is time for a change.

    Comments:

7. Jamie is eager to share. He has his hand up for every question. He is mildly mentally retarded and not a "deep thinker," but always has an answer to a question. His teacher is frustrated because sometimes the answers are "a little off base" and some of the other children are beginning to snicker. Jamie does not seem to care. He loves school, books, and reading. He wants to contribute to the class discussions about the books that are read in the classroom. His parents' expectations are high and they want the teacher to help Jaime to become a "deeper thinker."

    Comments:
    - prompting
    - study guides
    - partner working

8. Oh no! It has happened again. A fourth-grade teacher has just checked the readability level of her science and social studies books and they are written above fourth-grade level. How is she going to teach content area lessons to her students when the textbooks that she must use are sure to be too hard for most of the students in her classroom? What should she do now?

    Comments:
    - Realia
    - only focus on key concepts

ESL Anticipation/Reaction Guide

Before Presentation		After Presentation
	Students will learn to read faster if they possess those skills in their native language.	
	Once a child can hold a conversation in English he/she may be dropped from the ESL program.	
	During the early stages of English acquisition, grammar should not be emphasized.	
	It usually takes children 2–5 years to acquire a second language.	
	The strongest predictor of English language achievement is the amount of formal academic instruction in the native language.	
	It is important for groups of children from different languages and cultures to associate with each other to avoid ethnic, linguistic, and cultural isolation.	

Debating the Pros and Cons

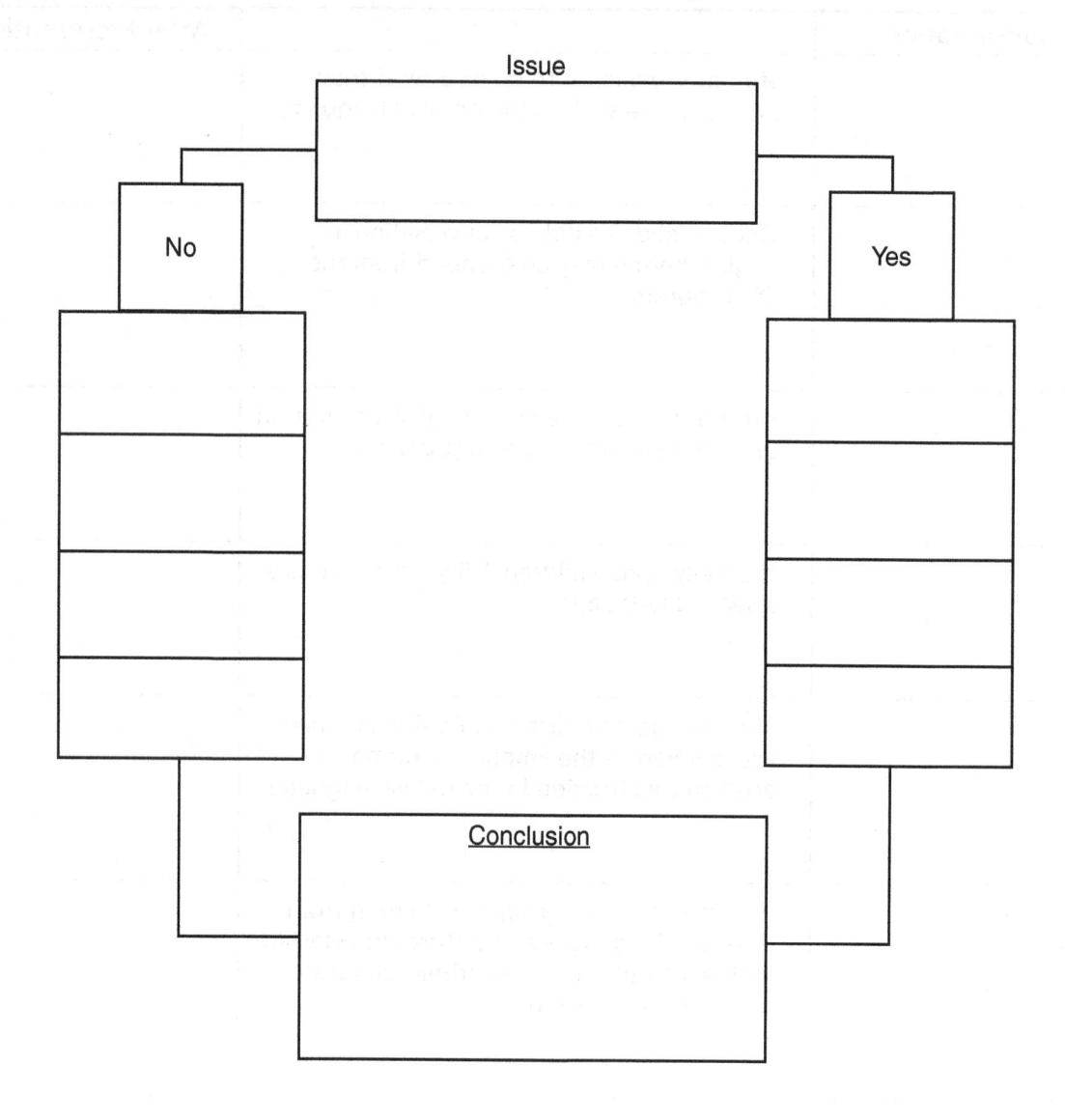

Issue

No

Yes

Conclusion

Adapted from Alverman, D. E. (1991). "The discussion web: A graphic aid for learning across the curriculum." *The Reading Teacher*, vol 45, 92–99.

Top 10 Things Teachers Can Do to Improve ELL Instruction

1. Enunciate clearly, but do not raise your voice. Add gestures and use visuals, manipulatives, and realia.

2. Write clearly, legibly, and in print.

3. Develop and maintain routines.

4. Repeat, summarize, rephrase, paraphrase, and review information frequently. Do not ask, "Do you understand?" Instead, have students demonstrate their understanding in order to show comprehension.

5. Initially avoid using idioms, slang words, and expressions of the "get verb."

6. Present new information in context of known information (background knowledge/BICS).

7. Announce lesson's objective, language objectives, and list instructions step by step.

8. Emphasize and explicitly (pre)teach key vocabulary words.

9. Attend to students' affective domains (lower Affective Filter).

10. Present information in a variety of ways!

"The Iceberg" Representation of Language Proficiency

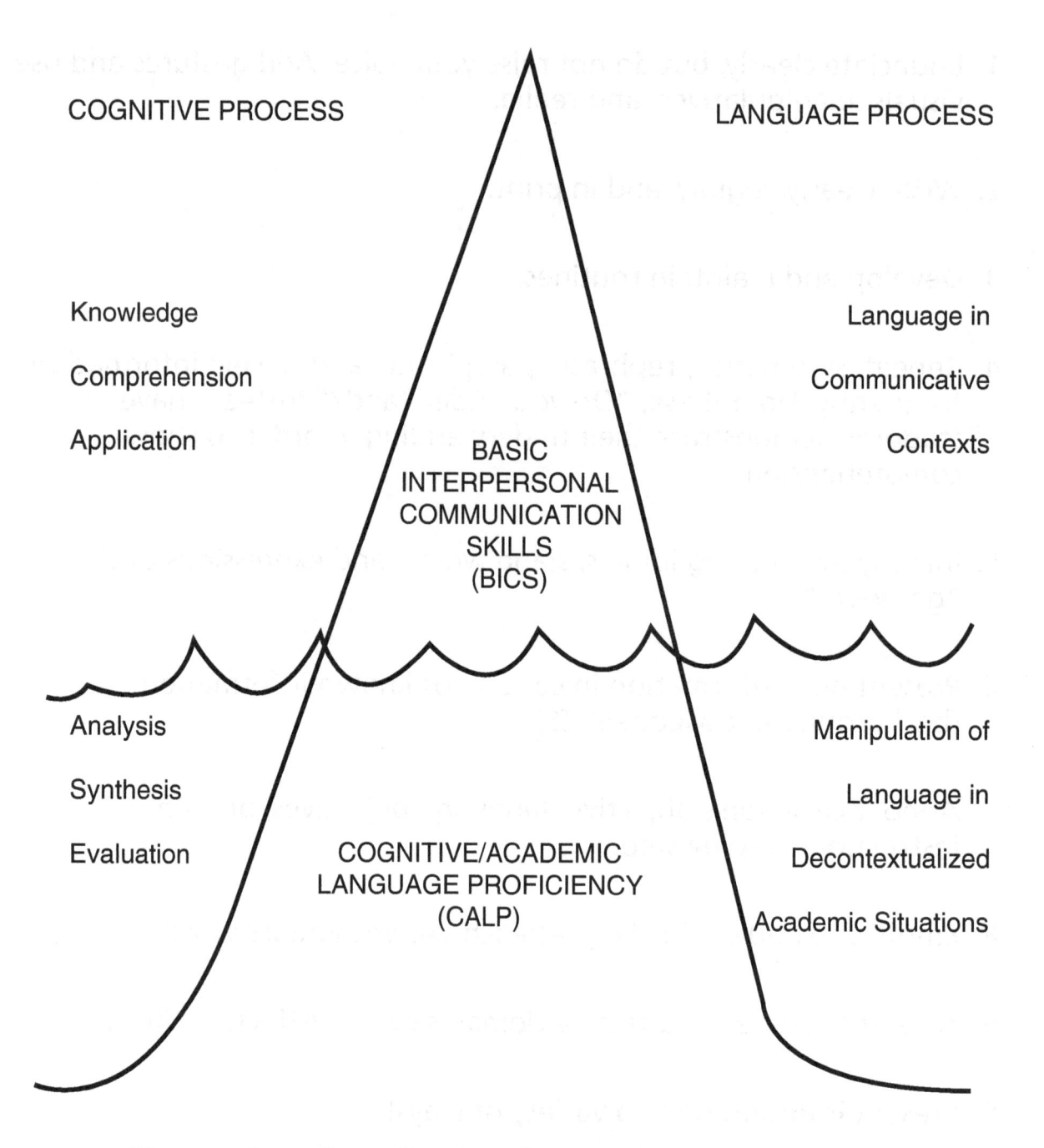

COGNITIVE PROCESS — LANGUAGE PROCESS

Knowledge

Comprehension

Application

Language in

Communicative

Contexts

BASIC INTERPERSONAL COMMUNICATION SKILLS (BICS)

Analysis

Synthesis

Evaluation

Manipulation of

Language in

Decontextualized

Academic Situations

COGNITIVE/ACADEMIC LANGUAGE PROFICIENCY (CALP)

Remember that the tip of an iceberg is only 10% and 90% lies below the surface.

Cummins, J. (1981). "The role of primary language development in promoting educational success for language minority students." *In Schooling and Language Minority Students: A Theoretical Framework.* Los Angeles: California State University, Evaluation, Dissemination, and Assessment Center.

How a Paragraph Looks to . . .

Beginning ELL Students:

Some _____ are more _____ during the day. They are called _____. _____ that are more _____ at _____ are called _____. They have _____ to _____ in the _____. We never see most of these _____. They are _____ during the day when we are _____.

Intermediate ELL Students:

Some animals are more _____ during the day. They are called _____. Animals that are more _____ at night are called _____. They have _____ to life in the dark. We never see most of these animals. They are _____ during the day when we are _____.

Advanced ELL Students:

Some animals are more active during the day. They are called diurnal. Animals that are more active at night are called nocturnal. They have adapted to life in the dark. We never see most of these animals. They are hiding during the day when we are awake.

Guidelines for Successful Reading Instruction for Young Second-Language Learners

Oral language

- Develop the childs's oral vocabulary to the point of basic communicative competence before attempting reading instruction.

- Continue to work on vocabulary training with the child well beyond the point of basic communicative competence to ensure adequate vocabulary for increasingly more difficult text.

- Provide opportunity for second-language children to converse in the classroom, being careful not to place undue emphasis on accurate speech.

Reading materials

- Remember that the child must know 90% to 95% of the vocabulary in the text before that text is used for reading instructional purposes.

- Use graded readers with second-language readers to ensure that text difficulty keeps pace with vocabulary development. But be sure to supplement with authentic literature first in read-alouds, then shared reading, and finally independent reading to ensure second-language readers are exposed to text that reflects natural speech.

- Encourage and provide opportunity for rereading of text.

"No Half Measure: Reading Instruction for Young Second-Language Learners" by Kimberly Lenters (2004), *The Reading Teacher,* Vol. 58, Issue 4, 328–336. Copyright © 2004 by International Reading Association. Reproduced with permission of International Reading Association in the format Textbook via Copyright Clearance Center.

Phonemic awareness

- Extend phonemic awareness training to include phonics instruction, using materials that teach sound-symbol correspondences in a multisensory and systematic manner.

Comprehension

- Use a language experience approach to provide meaningful materials the child is able to read.
- Pay attention to cultural biases in text and illustrations presented to young second-language learners.
- Fill in the missing cultural information when materials must be used that are culturally unfamiliar to the learner.
- When possible, use translations alongside English texts to enhance comprehension and support first-language reading skills. Parents and older siblings may be enlisted for this process.
- Allow students to respond to text in their first language.

First-language reading support

- Form strong home-school connections with the families of second-language learners.
- Value the child's first language.
- Find any means possible to ensure that the child receives reading instruction in his or her first language.

Read to Them

At first, ELL learners need to be systematically bathed in the sounds and meaning of English. Reading appropriate material in an appropriate manner with appropriate extension activities is a very efficient way of building their language competence. This will familiarize your ELL learners with the sound system, the grammatical patterns, and the rhythms of English; it will rapidly increase their vocabulary; and it will fan self-confidence and the desire to learn. Students find it very pleasurable and there is little threat.

Your time is short, so choose very short stories; or read just part of a story. Three minutes is great! This is where having the ELL student near your desk pays off, as you can sandwich in a mini-reading in a time slot too short to walk across the room in. You can also delegate the reading to a volunteer, a peer, or an upper-grade student.

Characteristics of appropriate material to read to beginning ELL learners:

- Copious illustrations with distinct pictures that clarify the text.
- Story plots that are action-based.
- Little text on each page.
- Text that may contain repetitive, predictable refrains.
- Majority of the vocabulary is high-frequency, useful words; simple sentence structures. Enlist the aid of the kindergarten teacher and your media center person.

The appropriate way to read to beginning ELL learners

- Point to the pictures as you mention an item in the text.

- Act out, dramatize, and provide hands-on objects and actions to make the story comprehensible.

- Read sentences at a slow-to-normal speed, enhancing the expression. Leave "digestion time" after each sentence or paragraph.

- On subsequent readings, point to the words in the text as you read them. This is essential for preliterate students and others who need to learn the left-to-right flow of our written language.

- "Big Books" are helpful if you have a large number of ELL students. They can see both text and illustrations easily.

Theatre of the Mind

1. _____

2. _____

3. _____

4. _____

5. _____

6. _____

Drs. William and Persida Himmele © Himmele 2002.

What reading teachers should know about ESL learners

Mary J. Drucker

Good teaching is teaching for all. These strategies will help English-language learners, but they will help typical learners as well.

According to figures released by the U.S. Census Bureau, the foreign-born population of the United States was 31.1 million in 2000. This figure is 57% more than the 1990 figure and represents 11.1% of the total population. Classrooms across the United States have English Language Learners (ELLs) who are learning to speak, read, and write in their new language. These students offer a rich resource of diversity that can enhance classroom dynamics. At the same time, they present a special challenge to classroom teachers and reading specialists alike. Out of nearly 3 million public school teachers surveyed by the National Center for Education Statistics, 41% report teaching limited English proficient (LEP) students, while only 12.5% have received eight or more hours of training (*NCELA Newsline Bulletin*, 2002).

There are some similarities between reading in a first language and reading in a second one. Accomplished readers in their first language tend to use many of the same strategies that successful native English-language readers do—skimming, guessing in context, reading for the gist of a text—when they are reading in a second language. But it would be a mistake to think that learning to read in a second language is simply a mapping process during which the reader uses the same set of strategies in precisely the same manner.

Support for students

In this article, I list some of the factors that can complicate the reading process for nonnative speakers of English and continue by offering suggestions and strategies that can support students as they strive to acquire English-language skills. The order of the factors presented is not hierarchical. Any one may be more important than the others, depending on the specific circumstance. I have included a Table that will give you an idea of when (before, during, or after a student reads) and for whom these activities have proven useful in the past. You may see the possibility of using an approach at a different time in your lesson, or for learners at different levels than those that I suggest. Feel free to adapt strategies for your particular situation if your learners differ in age or need, as they surely will.

I must add one pedagogical note here. You may begin to wonder, as you read, if a strategy described as being helpful for one category (developing cultural schema, for example) might be equally useful in another, such as helping a student gain academic proficiency. The answer is a resounding yes. The strategies linked to various categories are illustrative, not prescriptive. They represent best practices and so are often able to support students' reading development in a number of different areas.

Conversational versus academic proficiency

An English as a second language (ESL) learner may appear able to handle the demands of functioning in an English-only classroom because she or he is competent in a variety of school settings—talking with a friend in the corridor, playing ball on the playground, or speaking with the teacher one on one. It might seem natural to assume that a child learning English as a second language becomes fully fluent quickly. But researchers have found that, although ELLs can develop peer-appropriate conversational skills in about two years, developing academic proficiency in English can take much longer. Academic proficiency here refers to the ability not only to use language for reading and writing but also to acquire information in content areas. In most cases it takes an English-language learner as long as five to seven years to perform as well academically as native English-speaking peers (Collier & Thomas, 1999; Cummins, 1989). This lag occurs because the initial gap between native speakers and ELLs continues to persist. "Native English speakers are not sitting around waiting for ESL students to catch up. They are continuing to make 1 year's progress in 1 year's time in their English language development and in every school subject" (Collier & Thomas, 1999, p. 1). English-language learners have to gain more language proficiency each year than their native-speaking peers in order to catch up and close the gap.

What you can do in the classroom

In conversation, the setting, body language, facial expressions, gestures, intonation, and a variety of other cues help English-language learners understand meaning. Academic English has fewer contextual cues. You can help by providing context for your students before they begin reading text that may prove challenging for them. One helpful technique is previewing reading sections before students read. Chen and Graves (1998) provided a model for previewing that can easily be used in classrooms with ELLs. It is also an excellent strategy for native speakers whose reading skills are not yet on a par with their conversation skills. Previewing works well with students in grades 3 through 12.

Start by making a few statements or asking some rhetorical questions that hook the students' interest. Then, relate the passage students are going to read to something that is familiar to them. Next, provide a brief discussion question that will engage the students and, after that, provide an overview of the section they are about to read. Name the selection, introduce the characters, and describe the plot (up to, but not including, the climax). Last, direct the students to read the story and look for particular information. Chen and Graves (1998) provided the following example based on "Gift of the Magi" by O. Henry: "Now, read the story and find out why Della went into this shop, what she did there, and what happened later to the young couple on this Christmas Eve" (p. 571).

Providing so much preparation prior to reading is one way to ensure that students are receiving comprehensible input (Krashen, 1981). Comprehensible input is spoken or written language that is delivered at a level the child can understand. At the same time, the level should be enough of a challenge that the child needs to stretch just a bit above his or her current abilities. Krashen called this important level "I + 1," with "I" standing for input.

McCauley and McCauley (1992) suggested choral reading as a means of providing comprehensible input for ESL students. Choral reading involves the recitation of a poem or short text, along with motions and gestures that help the children dramatically act out the meaning. The many repetitions of reading a selection provide an opportunity to recycle the language, and the dramatic gestures and motions provide contextual clues about the poem's meaning. Choral reading is appropriate for students in kindergarten through sixth grade. For students in kindergarten or first grade, choral reading can be enhanced through the use of rebus symbols.

Orthography and phonology

Listening and reading are closely connected. At its most basic level, reading is the phonological decoding of written text, and written text is the representation of sounds heard when language is spoken. Ehri and Wilce (1985) separated native English-speaking kindergartners into groups according to their ability to read words. Prereaders had not yet learned to read at all; two other groups had learned to read only a few words or several different words. The children were taught to read words with two different kinds of spellings: simplified spellings that corresponded to sounds and visually distinctive words with spellings that did not correspond at all to their sound. Prereaders with no previous reading experience were able to read the visual spellings more easily than the phonetic spellings. The other children, with some experience reading, were more able to learn the phonetic spellings. In other words, children who had begun learning how to read had already started moving toward an orientation incorporating sound/symbol correspondence.

Researchers have also noted that differences between languages with deep orthographic structures (having many irregular sound-letter correspondences) versus shallow ones (having mainly regular sound-letter correspondences) might cause difficulty for some nonnative readers of English (Grabe, 1991; Paulesu et al., 2001; Wade-Woolley, 1999). Paulesu et al. examined the connection between dyslexia and cultural conventions in orthography. The researchers found that although dyslexia is a genetic disorder, its occurrence appears unevenly distributed across languages. For example, the prevalence of dyslexia in Italy is about half that of the United States. Beginning with the accepted assumption that there was a causal link between phonological processing deficits and brain abnormality, researchers looked at the orthography of various languages in relation to their phonetic material. They concluded that dyslexics in languages such as Italian that have a shallow orthography may be less affected in their ability to read. The dyslexia, in effect, remains hidden. In deep orthography languages such as English, literacy impairments may be aggravated.

What you can do in the classroom

Shared reading provides English-language learners with an opportunity to hear language while observing its corresponding phonological representation. McCarrier, Pinnell and Fountas (2000) defined shared reading as "you and your students read[ing] together from a single, enlarged text" (p. 18). Naturally, the writing should be large enough to be seen from a distance, and the text should be positioned so that it is in clear view of all of the children. Aside from its obvious support for learners of English who need help in word-by-word matching, shared reading also helps children learn left-to-right directionality (McCarrier et al.). This may give extra dividends for ELLs whose native orthography differs from English's left-to-right, top-to-bottom directionality. Shared reading can be used in the early elementary years, from kindergarten through third grade. As always, choosing reading materials with an appropriate reading level is a critical factor. For kindergarten and first-grade students, rebus symbols can be used in place of some or most of the text.

Li and Nes (2001) found that paired reading was also useful in helping ESL students read more fluently and accurately. They paired ELLs with a "skilled reader" who read a portion of text aloud while the language learner read along. The language learner then reread the same text aloud. The researchers found that paired reading was an effective intervention that improved the students' fluency in reading aloud, as well as their pronunciation. Paired reading works well with students who have developed some independent social skills and task follow-through. In general, students in grades 3 through 8 can pair-read successfully. Younger students require more structure.

Studies of learning-disabled students have found that children benefit from the simultaneous listening and reading of audiotaped stories (Conte & Humphreys, 1989; Janiak, 1983). Rasinski (1990) found that listening while reading was effective in improving reading fluency. Casbergue and Harris (1996) noted that audiobooks "provide a means for engaging youngsters who are not habituated to print" (p. 4).

Although the typical ESL student is not learning disabled, the sound/symbol correspondence in these studies is interesting. Consider providing ELLs with books and corresponding audiotapes. Books and tapes work well with any student who can independently read text (grades 2 through 12). For kindergarten and first-grade students, books and tapes provide an opportunity to hear the sounds of English as well as learn basic literacy practices like page turning, tracking left to right, and making meaningful connections between words and illustrations. The tapes can be recorded by the teacher or by other students in the class. Providing exposure to books and corresponding tapes gives language learners an opportunity to simultaneously hear the sounds and see the corresponding graphic representation. The word *simultaneous* is the key here. Students need many opportunities to both hear the spoken word and see its graphic representation. Children who have listened to and read a story many times can be encouraged to read aloud along with the tape while listening to the story.

Cultural differences and schema

Schema theory holds that comprehending a text involves an interaction between the reader's background knowledge and the text itself (Carrell & Eisterhold, 1983). In other words, comprehension requires more than linguistic knowledge. Consider the following passage offered by Eskey (2002): "It was the day of the big party. Mary wondered if Johnny would like a kite. She ran to her bedroom, picked up her piggy bank, and shook it. There was no sound" (p. 6). Eskey asked us to consider a series of questions about the reading:

- when the story took place—past, present, or future;
- what Mary wondered;
- the meaning of *would*;
- the definition of *kite*;
- the definition of *piggy bank*;
- the nature of the party in the text;
- if Mary and Johnny are adults or children;
- how the kite is related to the party;
- why Mary shook her piggy bank; and
- what Mary's big problem was.

The point that Eskey made with this exercise is that the first five questions posed can be answered by directly searching the text, as long as the reader knows the vocabulary and English structures. The second five questions, however, are far more difficult to answer unless the reader possesses the schema of a child's birthday party in the United States. The questions cannot be answered without this specific cultural information. A native speaker of English, however, is easily able to construct a correct interpretation of the text.

Other studies have noted the importance of cultural differences and schema. Carrell (1987) studied 52 ESL students: 28 Muslim Arabs and 24 Catholic Hispanics. Each student read two different texts, one with a Muslim orientation and the other with a Catholic orientation. The researcher found that the students better remembered and comprehended those texts most similar to their native cultures.

Droop and Verhoeven (1998) studied third graders becoming literate in Dutch both as a first and second language. The children read three different kinds of texts: texts that referred to Dutch culture, texts that referred to the cultures of the immigrant children, and neutral texts. It is not surprising that the researchers found that the children had better reading comprehension and reading efficiency with texts that were culturally familiar.

What you can do in the classroom

When possible, choose texts that will match the cultural schemata and background knowledge of your English-language learners. Folk tales that are translations of stories children may have heard in their native language are especially helpful. Students will be able to relate more easily to books that depict characters that are similar to them. Two concept books for kindergarten and first-grade children, *Red Is a Dragon* and *Round Is a Mooncake* (Thong, 2000, 2002), have delightful illustrations of Asian children and simple language introducing colors and shapes. *The Ugly Vegetables* (Lin, 1999) is a picture book suitable for grades 1 through 4. It tells the story of a young Chinese girl who feels different from her American friends because of the strange vegetables her mother grows in their garden. When the vegetables ripen, her mother makes a delicious soup that everyone in the neighborhood enjoys, and the girl learns to value her culture as a result.

Another picture book good for first through third grade, *The Iguana Brothers* (Johnston, 1995), tells the tale of two lizard siblings in English, with an occasional word in Spanish. The Spanish vocabulary can be easily understood through context by native English speakers. However, the Spanish language and culturally appropriate illustrations may provide native Spanish speakers with a cultural context that makes the meanings that much more accessible.

Multicultural literature is a positive addition to the classroom for all students in all grades, from kindergarten through high school. Native speakers of English "need to be familiar with quality literature which can give the reader a realistic look at those many cultures" (McDonald, 1996, p. 1). In increasingly diverse U.S. classrooms, it is critical for books to reflect the cultural backgrounds of all students. Shioshita (1997) has culled information from several sources on how to select quality multicultural literature and offers the following tips:

- Books should be accurate and contain current information.
- Books should not reinforce stereotypes, but rather they should reflect the experiences of individuals.
- Illustrations should realistically depict individuals of different ethnicities.
- Stories should be appealing.

Another way to be certain that students fully share the context of the material they are reading is through the Language Experience Approach (LEA; Rigg, 1981). Language learners of all ages enjoy this approach, but in a classroom containing native English speakers LEA is generally more successful with students in grades 1 through 3. LEA involves having students tell the story of an experience they have had. The teacher acts as scribe, writing down the words so that the students can see what they look like. If the students have had a shared experience, such as a field trip or a visitor to the classroom, parts of the story come from all of the students in the class. After a story has been completed, the teacher can copy it onto a large sheet of chart paper so that students can practice reading it together. The rationale for using LEA can be summed up in these lines:

> What I can think about I can talk about.
>
> What I can say I can write.
>
> What I can write I can read.
>
> I can read what I write and what other people write for me to read.
>
> (R. Van Allen & G. Halvoren, as cited in Cantoni-Harvey, 1992, p. 178)

Interactive writing (McCarrier et al., 2000), in which children share the pen with their teacher, also allows children to share in the writing of a text that grows from their own experiences. In interactive writing, the teacher and the children negotiate the meaning of the text together and work together to produce it; the children are invited to contribute to the writing of the text on the basis of their instructional needs.

> *The idea is to help children attend to powerful examples that can enable them to learn something about the writing process that they can incorporate into their own writing. As children gain control of the process, the examples and areas of focus shift. (McCarrier et al., p. 11)*

Interactive writing has been successful in the early grades, generally first through third.

Vocabulary

On a very basic level, vocabulary is critical to the reading process. Fluent first-language readers have large recognition vocabularies. There have been numerous studies attempting to quantify the actual number of words second-language readers need to know in order to comprehend a text. It is not surprising that some researchers have found that second-language learners need approximately the same number of words in their lexicon as first-language readers (Goulden, Nation, & Read, 1990). This need presents a particular challenge because of the large amount of prerequisite information ELLs must learn in order to be at a reading level comparable to their peers. W. Nagy & P. Herman (as cited in Bell, 1998) found that students between 3rd and 12th grade learn up to 3,000 new words each year. Classroom teachers are simply unable to teach this amount of vocabulary item by item.

In addition, many of the standard vocabulary-teaching approaches have been ineffective with ESL learners. Freeman and Freeman (2000) noted that although ELLs enjoy vocabulary exercises, they have trouble applying the information they memorize in context. According to Yeung (1999),

> *Given a separate glossary, when readers encounter an unfamiliar word, they need to leave the text, turn to the vocabulary list, temporarily store its meaning, and then revert to the text and try to incorporate the meaning into the text. (p. 197)*

Yeung posited that the difficulty with providing students with preteaching vocabulary exercises or glossaries creates a cognitive load that splits the learner's attention. He found that when definitions are placed next to the challenging lexical items, students were better able to learn the meanings of unfamiliar words. He suggested that in this integrated format, students' attention is not split, and the cognitive load is lowered.

What you can do in the classroom

Although we cannot edit the materials our students use so that vocabulary definitions are integrated with the text, it is possible to encourage students to write word meanings on labels that are placed in the margins or as near the challenging item as possible. This may help to reduce the cognitive load and enhance vocabulary acquisition. Labeling tends to be more successful with students who have a greater ability to work independently, generally grade 4 through high school. We can also explain meanings, or add synonyms for words that seem to cause (or seem likely to cause) difficulty for some of the students, as challenging words appear during the shared reading exercise described earlier.

Schunk (1999) suggested a different approach to vocabulary acquisition. She found that elementary school children (kindergarten through grade 5) who engaged in singing as a form of language rehearsal, paired with sign language, improved on receptive identification of targeted vocabulary. This approach is reminiscent of a language teaching methodology known as total physical response (TPR). TPR is "built around the coordination of speech and action; it attempts to teach language through physical (motor) activity" (Richards & Rodgers, 1998, p. 87). Encouraging children to act out songs such as "Itsy Bitsy Spider" and having them play games associated with language like Simon Says are other examples of this approach. Having children physically act out songs, poems, or readings—all forms of TPR methodology—is an effective way to support vocabulary development.

Schmitt and Carter (2000) suggested narrow reading as an effective method for developing vocabulary. In narrow reading, learners read authentic writing about the same topic in a number of different texts. By doing this, students are exposed to a common body of vocabulary. In this way, these words are recycled and ultimately integrated with the learner's vocabulary. There is not clear agreement about the number of times that a language learner must encounter a new lexical term before it is actually learned, but Zahar, Cobb, and Spada (2001) found that estimates range between 6 and 20 times, depending on the context in which exposure to the word occurs. Depending on the materials available, students in grades 2 or 3 all the way up through high school can engage in narrow reading.

Schmitt and Carter (2000) suggested the following kinds of narrow-reading activities to support vocabulary acquisition.

- Collect newspaper stories on a continuing topic for students to read. Be certain each story is one that will appeal to them.
- Ask students to bring in magazines on subjects they like. Have them read several articles from the magazines.
- Use the Internet—there is a wide variety of texts available on almost any topic.
- Assign books for the students to read. The vocabulary in any given novel tends to recycle.
- Have students read texts written by a single author.

Finally, do not underestimate the power of read-alouds in supporting vocabulary development. Freeman and Freeman (2000) pointed to a study in which teachers read aloud a story to students three times a day for a week. Group vocabulary scores rose by 40%. "The key was finding interesting books and coaching teachers to use reading techniques such as pointing to pictures, gesturing, and paraphrasing . . . to be sure students understood the story" (p. 123).

Many possible approaches

In classrooms that are becoming increasingly diverse, culturally relevant teaching is an important component of literacy instruction. Culturally relevant teaching is "the kind of teaching that is designed not merely to *fit* the school culture to the students' culture but also to *use* student culture as the basis for helping students understand themselves and others, structure social interactions, and conceptualize knowledge" (Ladson-Billings, 2000, p. 142).

Effective literacy instruction is not simply a collection of strategies and approaches that will help English-language learners succeed in mainstream classrooms. The environment in which ELLs study and learn is at least as important as the methods, strategies, and approaches you may choose to employ. Using a culturally relevant teaching approach means that students' second languages can be viewed as an additive to the classroom environment, rather than as a deficit that needs to be remedied. Realize that academic language proficiency in a second language takes a long time to develop. To facilitate that process, permit students to use their native languages when necessary (Nichols, Rupley, & Webb-Johnson, 2000). The classroom needs to be a validating environment for all students. Williams (2001) suggested asking yourself, "Would I want to be a student in my classroom?" (p. 754).

The strategies listed in this article are not intended to be prescriptive solutions for particular issues in literacy development. They are a few of many possible approaches that can be useful for all students, both native speakers of English as well as English-language learners in the classroom. Like native speakers, "Second language learners benefit from reading programs that incorporate a range of contexts, both social and functional, and in which reading begins, develops, and is used as a means of communication" (Nichols et al., 2000, p. 2).

It is also important to remember the concept of Krashen's I + 1 (1981), mentioned earlier. Texts must be at a level appropriate to the student's ability. Recall also that academic language proficiency takes much longer to develop than conversational proficiency. "In other words, encourage students to read at their reading level—not at their oral proficiency level" (Williams, 2001, p. 751). There is nothing like reading to promote reading. "Read aloud to students every day. This practice supports language development . . . as well as literacy development" (p. 751).

Finally, give students plenty of opportunities to read independently. "People learn to read, and to read better, by reading" (Eskey, 2002, p. 8). Students learn to read well when they are engaged in reading materials that are not only at an appropriate level but also interesting and relevant to them.

References

Bell, T. (1998, December). Extensive reading: Why? And how? *The Internet TESOL Journal, IV*(12). Retrieved March 7, 2001, from http://www.aitech.ac.ip/~iteslj/Articles/Bell-Reading.html

Cantoni-Harvey, G. (1992). Facilitating the reading process. In P. A. Richard-Amato & M. A. Snow (Eds.), *The multicultural classroom* pp. 175–197). Reading, MA: Addison Wesley.

Carrell, P., & Eisterhold, J. C. (1983). Schema theory and ESL reading pedagogy. *TESOL Quarterly, 18,* 441–469.

Carrell, P. L. (1987). Content and formal schemata in ESL reading: *TESOL Quarterly, 21,* 461–481.

Casbergue, R. M., & Harris, H. H. (1996). Listening and literacy; Audio-books in the reading program. *Reading Horizons, 37,* 48–59.

Chen, H. S., & Graves, M. F. (1998). Previewing challenging reading selections for ESL students. *Journal of Adolescent & Adult Literacy, 41,* 570–572.

Collier, V. P., & Thomas, W. P. (1999). Making U.S. schools effective for English language learners, Part 1. *TESOL Matters, 9*(4), 1–6.

Conte, R., & Humphreys, R. (1989). Repeated readings using audio-taped materials enhances oral reading in children with reading difficulties. *Journal of Communication Disorders, 22* 65–79.

Cummins, J. (1989). *Empowering minority students.* Sacramento, CA: California Association for Bilingual Education.
Droop, M., & Verhoeven L. (1998). Background knowledge, linquistic complexity, and second-language reading comprehension. *Journal of Literacy Research, 30,* 253–271.
Ehri, L. C., & Wilce, L. S. (1985). Movement into reading: Is the first stage of printed word learning visual or phonetic? *Reading Research Quarterly, 20,* 163–179.
Eskey, D. E. (2002). Reading and the teaching of L2 reading. *TESOL Journal, 11*(1), 5–9.
Freeman, D. E., & Freeman, Y. S. (2000). *Teaching reading in multilingual classrooms.* Portsmouth, NH: Heinemann.
Goulden, R., Nation, P., & Read, J. (1990). How large can a receptive vocabulary be? *Applied Linguistics, 11,* 341–363.
Grabe, W. (1991). Current developments in second language reading research. *TESOL Quarterly, 25,* 375–406.
Janiak, R. (1983). Listening/reading: An effective learning combination. *Academic Therapy, 19,* 205–211.
Johnston, T. (1995). *The iguana brothers.* New York: Blue Sky Press.
Krashen, S. (1981). *Second language acquisition and second language learning.* Oxford, England: Pergamon.
Ladson-Billings, G. (2000). Reading between the lines and beyond the pages: A culturally relevant approach to literacy teaching. In M. Gallego & A. Hollingsworth (Eds.), *What counts as literacy?: Challenging the school standard* (pp. 139–151). New York: Teachers College Press.
Li, D., & Nes, S. L. (2001). Using paired reading to help ESL students become fluent and accurate readers. *Reading Improvement, 38*(2), 50–61.
Lin, G. (1999). *The ugly vegetables.* Watertown, MA: Charlesbridge.
McCarrier, A., Pinnell, G. S., & Fountas, I. C. (2000). Interactive writing: *How language and literacy come together, K–2.* Portsmouth, NH: Heinemann.
McCauley, J. K., & McCauley, D. S. (1992). Using choral reading to promote language learning for ESL students. *The Reading Teacher, 45,* 526–533.
McDonald, J. (1996, Spring). A multicultural literature bibliography. *The ALAN Review, 23.* Retrieved July 20, 2002, from *http://scholar.lib.vt.edu/ejournals/ALAN/spring96/mcdonald.html*
NCELA Newsline Bulletin, (2002, June 11). NCES survey: Over 40 percent of U.S. teachers teach LEPs. Retrieved June 11, 2002, from *http://www.ncbe.gwu.edu/newsline/soos/0611.htm*
Nichols, W. D., Rupley, W. H, & Webb-Johnson, G. (2000). Teacher's role in providing culturally responsive literacy instruction. *Reading Horizons, 41*(1), 1–18.
Paulesu, E., Demonet, J. F., Faxio, F., WcCrory, E., Chanoine, V., Brunswick, N., et al. (2001). Dyslexia: Cultural diversity and biological unity. *Science, 291,* 2165–2167.
Rasinski, T. (1990). Effects of repeated reading and listening-while-reading on reading fluency. *Journal of Educational Research, 83,* 147–150.
Richards, J., & Rodgers, T. (1998). *Approaches and methods in language teaching.* New York: Cambridge University Press.
Rigg, P. (1981). Beginning to read in English the LEA way. In C. W. Twyford, W. Diehl, & K. Feathers (Eds.), *Reading English as a second language: Moving from theory* (pp. 81–90). Bloomington, IN: Indiana University Press.
Schmitt, N., & Carter, R. (2000). The lexical advantages of narrow reading for second language learners. *TESOL Journal, 9*(1), 4–9.
Schunk, H. A. (1999). The effect of singing paired with signing on receptive vocabulary skills of elementary ESL students. *The Journal of Music Therapy, 36,* 110–124.
Shioshita, J. (1997). *Beyond good intentions: Selecting multi-cultural literature.* Oakland, CA: Action Alliance for Children. Retrieved July 20, 2002, from *http://www.4children.org/news/9-97mlit.htm*
Thong, R. (2000). *Round is a mooncake.* San Francisco: Chronicle Books.
Thong, R. (2002). *Red is a dragon.* San Francisco: Chronicle Books.
Wade-Woolley, L. (1999). First language influences on second language word reading: All roads lead to Rome. *Language Learning, 49,* 447–471.
Williams, J. A. (2001). Classroom conversations: Opportunities to learn for ESL students in mainstream classrooms, *The Reading Teacher, 54,* 750–757.
Yeung, A. S. (1999). Cognitive load and learner expertise: Split-attention and redundancy effects in reading comprehension tasks with vocabulary definitions. *The Journal of Experimental Education, 67,* 197–217.
Zahar, R., Cobb, T., & Spada, N. (2001). Acquiring vocabulary through reading: Effects of frequency and contextual richness. *Canadian Modern Language Review, 57,* 541–572.